Spirit up
the People

PHOTOGRAPHS BY TAYLOR LEWIS, JR
TEXT BY JOANNE YOUNG

UNDER THE AUSPICES OF
THE NORTH CAROLINA
BICENTENNIAL FOUNDATION

OXMOOR HOUSE, INC • BIRMINGHAM

NORTH CAROLINA ✶ THE FIRST TWO HUNDRED YEARS

Spirit up the People

Library of Congress Catalog Number: 75-17098

Copyright © 1975 by Oxmoor House, Inc., P.O. Box 2463,
Birmingham, Alabama 35202.
All rights reserved.
First edition published 1975.

Printed in the United States of America.

Published by Oxmoor House, Inc.
Book Division of The Progressive Farmer Company.

Mary Whitfield, *Managing Editor*

Taylor Lewis, Jr., *Photographer*
Joanne Young, *Author*
Pace Barnes, *Editor*
Bob Reed, *Designer*
Jeffery Crow, *Historical Consultant*
Kurt Lang, *Cartographer*

You are appointed to the command of a Corps
of Light Infantry, a detachment of Militia
and Lieutenant Colonel Washington's Regiment of
Light Dragoons. . . .
The object of this detachment is to give
protection to that part of the country and
spirit up the people.

From General Nathanael Greene to Daniel Morgan
at Charlotte, North Carolina, December 16, 1780.

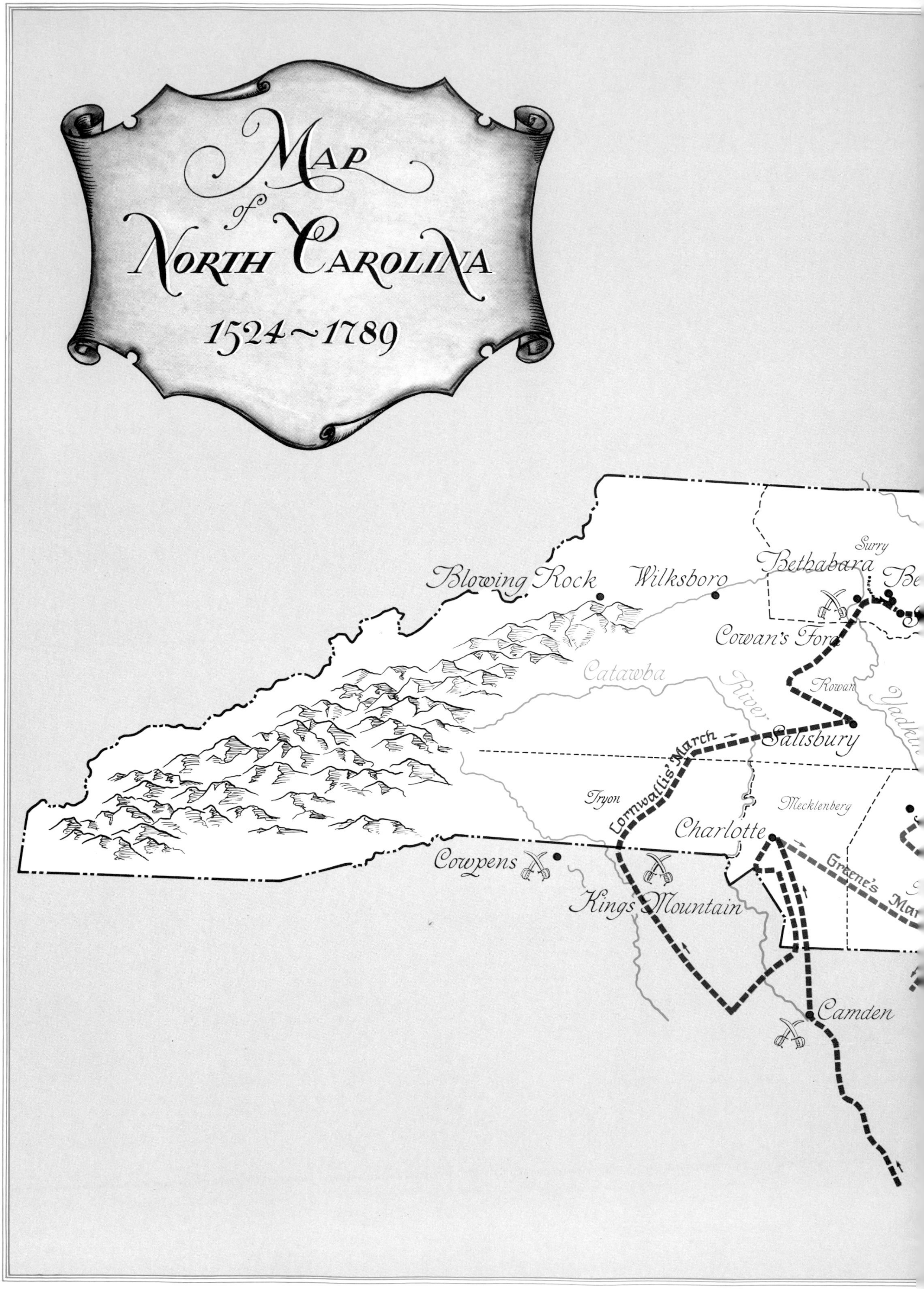

MAP of NORTH CAROLINA

1524~1789

Blowing Rock

Wilksboro

Bethabara

Surry

Be

Cowan's Ford

Catawba

River

Rowan

Yadki

Salisbury

Cornwallis' March

Tryon

Mecklenberg

Charlotte

Greene's Mar

Cowpens

Kings Mountain

Camden

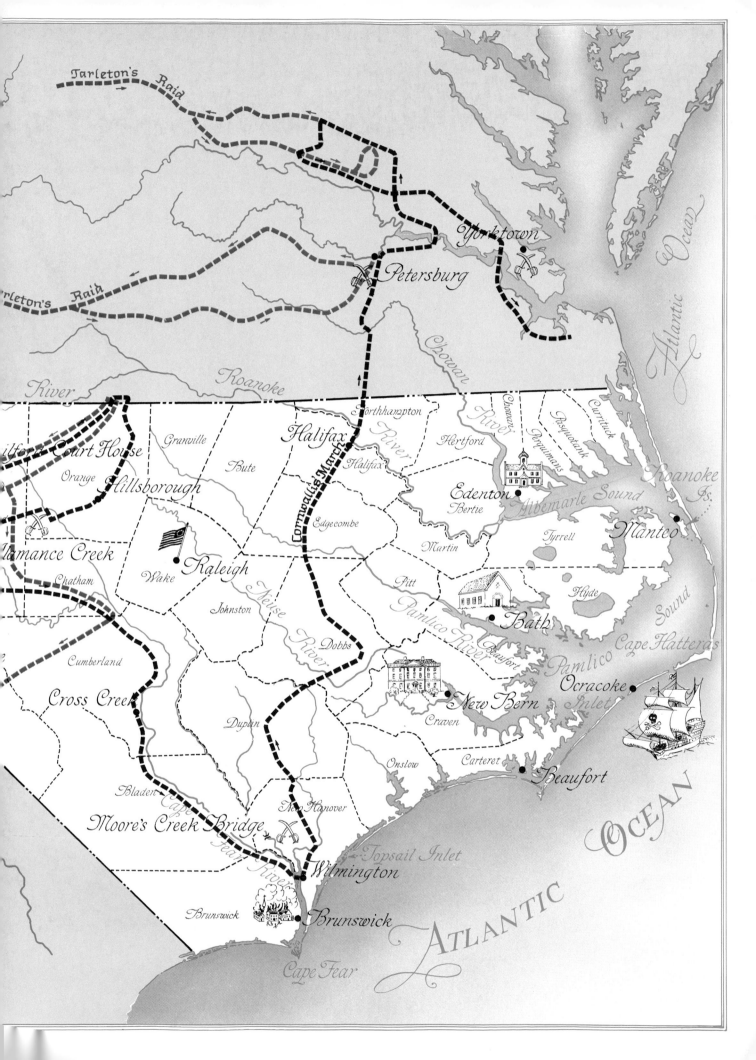

Tarleton's Raid

Tarleton's Raid

Yorktown

Petersburg

Chowan

Roanoke   Roanoke

River   River

Northhampton

Halifax

Chowan   Currituck

Hertford   Pasquotank

Perquimans

Granville   Halifax   River

Cornwallis March   Edenton   Roanoke

Guilford Court House   Bute   Bertie   Albemarle Sound   Is.

Orange   Hillsborough   Edgecombe   Manteo

Alamance Creek   Tyrrell

Chatham   Martin   Hyde

Raleigh   Pitt

Wake   Pamlico River   Sound

Johnston   Neuse   Bath   Cape Hatteras

Cumberland   River   Dobbs   Beaufort   Ocracoke

Craven   New Bern   Inlet

Cross Creek   Duplin   Pamlico

Carteret   Beaufort

Bladen   Cape   New Hanover   Onslow

Moore's Creek Bridge   Fear   Topsail Inlet

River   Wilmington   OCEAN

Brunswick   Brunswick   ATLANTIC

Cape Fear

Atlantic Ocean

They were sailing west. For a number of days now a new mildness in the ocean air had warmed the Florentine captain's bones. He had never fully adjusted to the colder climate of France from which he had sailed. In the early days of this voyage the Atlantic wind, even on a sunny day, had chilled him more severely than any winter storm at home. Now the very color of the water seemed a gentler blue, whereas even a week ago it had been a roiling gray green that added to a general feeling of cold and misery.

The warmth had lifted the spirits of the crew as it had their captain's. Some sense of change in their luck along with the change in the ocean current and the weather had per-meated them. Often, even without orders, a seaman would scramble up the mainmast on the pretense of checking the rigging. Then he would scan the horizon with an eager eye instead of desperately straining for some glimpse of land as he had done for the past weeks.

Yesterday, Verra-zano, standing on the forecastle, had sworn he spotted a land bird off to starboard, but the small black speck in the sky was gone too fast for him to be sure. He prided himself that he could smell land even before he sighted it. Now the subtle scent of vegeta-tion and sun-baked sand hit him, a heart-lifting relief from the familiar reeking of human bod-ies too closely cramped together and the perpet-ual briny smell which had buoyed him so at their sailing. Today would be the day!

The cry went up even sooner than he had expected. A thin veil of morning mist prevented him from confirming for endless minutes the lookout's sighting. Then in an instant the mist cleared, and the Florentine saw, too, the tiny undulation to the west, the low gray silhouette that barely broke the horizon line, the sweet sight of land!

Cheering men crammed the rail causing the ship to list dangerously. In order to balance the ship, Verrazano had to order them back to their stations. But they had seen an island—there was no doubt of that. The sun rose higher. Gradually the gray of the approach-ing land turned to ribbons of white and green in the blue sea that lapped around it.

His heart leaped. His rapid breathing almost suffocated him. Perhaps he had found the fabled Northwest Passage that had eluded even the great Magellan! He would sail past this island, on through the blue sea, and before him would lie the riches of the East!

The words of the Genoese explorer Christopher Columbus that three decades ago had excited all Europe—together with the boy Giovanni da Verrazano—throbbed in his ears above the pounding of the surf on the white beach: "The gate to the gold and pearls is now open," Columbus had written, "and precious stones, spices, and a thousand other things may surely be expected."

A flock of gulls, wheeling and soaring with cries that the Florentine took as shrieks of welcome, dipped low over the ship's wake and glided up and over her sails. The flag of Francis I of France whipped in the breeze—never more proudly, Verrazano thought ecstatically.

"It is found! It is found!" His heart sang as his ship cut through the narrowing sea toward the shore that one day would be named Cape Fear in that land that would be Carolina.

The next few weeks were like a dream to Verrazano, filled with adventure and experiences that few men ever know. To walk in a new world, to wake each morning and see stretched out before him a land which no European had ever seen, to watch the sun rise above a mist-draped island where exotic birds rose in clouds above golden marshes—it was enough to intoxicate a man with sheer wonder.

However, he discovered even Eden had its dangers. His first anchorage proved to be in treacherous hidden shoals that ran out some twenty miles from the land, so he decided to sail up the coast to a better harbor. Soon Verrazano felt certain that his first intuition that the Northwest Passage lay before him was correct. Sailing through not just one but several inlets, he confirmed for himself that the Pacific Ocean lay just beyond the land.

He also encountered the race of people who inhabited this country: they were strong and graceful of build, with smooth copper-colored skin and long black hair. They were also, he noted after a group of them rescued a sailor who carelessly fell overboard, "very courteous and gentle."

He could scarcely wait to sail home and tell the wonderful news of his discovery to the king. What joy there would be among the merchants of Lyon who had backed his voyage! Sure that his leave-taking was only temporary, he set his homeward course. In his mind's eye he was already taking on provisions for his imminent return and an even longer stay on these shores. And, of course, the next time he would have sufficient supplies on board to sail on westward to the Orient.

But war clouds had gathered over France during his absence, and to his amazement, Verrazano found Francis I so occupied with military matters that he gave scant attention to the Florentine's glowing report on his discoveries.

It was the English Sea Dogs, more than half a century later, who brought about a serious attempt to follow up exploration of the North Carolina coast with settlement. Chagrined that their only share of New World treasure was what they could capture from well-laden Spanish ships, the British realized colonization was the only answer.

In April 1584 Sir Walter Raleigh sent from England two ships "well furnished with men and victuals" to explore the site for a future American colony. In command were Philip Amadas and Arthur Barlowe, and with them sailed an experienced Portuguese pilot Simon Ferdinándo. Another member of their party was a remarkable artist John White whose brush,

First sighted by Verrazano in 1524,
the area that became Cape Fear
remains beautiful with lush semitropical flora
and bountiful wildlife.
Lady slippers were found on the forest floor
then as now.

The explorer
came ashore somewhere near Orton Plantation
where these photographs
were taken.

Raleigh reasoned, could graphically record the most minute detail of the New World and draw maps of it to supplement written reports.

The English expedition sighted land on the fourth of July somewhere along the Outer Banks of North Carolina. A little more than a week later they came ashore near Roanoke Island and under Raleigh's charter took possession of the land for their Queen. Marveling at its beauty as Verrazano had done, they immediately began to explore the area. Then Barlowe with his pen and White with his brush and water colors set to work to record the summertime of these islands.

A few days later they received a visit from Granganimeo, the brother of Wingina, chief of the Roanoke Island Indians who were members of the Secotan tribe. In wary curiosity as well as in courtesy, Barlowe and seven others returned his visit soon afterward, taking a small boat across the sound to the Indian's palisaded village. They were hospitably treated, and John White could hardly wait to return there with his palette and paper.

This entire expedition was an experience White had never anticipated when, at middle age, he went his somewhat uneventful way along the London streets to and from his daily work with the Painters and Stainers Guild. An ocean voyage to explore an unknown land had never entered his mind until one of Raleigh's men approached him with the offer. White was married and had a teenage daughter, Eleanor, and his family and his painting filled his life — or so he had thought. Overnight his horizon widened to include limitless possibilities.

John White was a realistic painter, and he turned his keen powers of observation to reporting accurately the natural form and energy of the New World's wildlife, plants, and people. What he felt, he communicated in his art; what he felt as he roamed the sandy shores of the Outer Banks was a vigorous, swelling enthusiasm.

On even the warmest day fresh salt breezes exhilarated him. Wherever he looked there were live oaks and even pines that to his artist's eye seemed sculpted by the wind into marvelously intricate shapes. Together with Barlowe, he noted the lushness of the grapes that hung in succulent clusters from vines that covered sandy dunes and climbed the highest cedar trees. They marveled at the water birds and the game that abounded in the wood. One day they

Spanish moss is a familiar sight along the Cape Fear coast and has provided the atmosphere for much legend.

watched an Indian fisherman pull in fish after fish until his canoe was almost too low in the water to be paddled to shore.

Knowing Raleigh's desire to match Spanish riches, Barlowe mentioned in his report a shiny metal he had noticed—whether it was copper or gold he was unable to tell—and the glossy skins of deer and buffalo which the English had received in trade from the Indians. From King Wingina they obtained a handsome pearl bracelet to take back to their sponsor. Barlowe reported that the Indians were "gentle, loving, and faithful."

As far as it went, their report to London was highly accurate. In summertime there were no hurricanes, no worries about food—with nature's largess apparent on every side—no jealous guarding of hunting grounds nor dwindling supplies of dried Indian corn and other food that in winter must be made to last.

Raleigh was impressed with the findings they presented to him in London and by his meetings with the two Indians, Wanchese and Manteo, who had returned with the English party. Soon thereafter Queen Elizabeth named the newly explored land Virginia in modest recognition of herself, the Virgin Queen.

By April Raleigh had fitted out seven ships for a return voyage. In this fleet sailed at least 300 soldiers and specialists, in addition to the ships' crews. This was to be a military expedition headed by his cousin Sir Richard Grenville, a veteran mariner and privateer, and with him sailed a number of distinguished relatives and friends. Along with these noblemen came an eminent scientist Thomas Hariot, who had learned the rudiments of the Indian language from Wanchese and Manteo during the winter and in return had taught them English. There was also a group of skilled craftsmen including miners and metalworkers, bricklayers and blacksmiths. Philip Amadas, John White, and Simon Ferdinándo, the pilot, also returned with the expedition.

From the latter part of June until late in July, they explored various islands along the Outer Banks and the nearby mainland. They were skilled in the arts of war and survival and confident of the effectiveness of the sword. While the first expedition had come in peace, to explore and to report, they had come to conquer. When they arrived at the village of Aquascogoc, Grenville presented his token gifts to the chief and served a lavish meal—possibly one such as he normally served the noblemen in his own company "on plate of silver and gold." He expected the Indian ruler to understand the European standards by which certain objects were intended for presents and certain others for their temporary use only. Since the red men drew no such fine distinctions, it is not surprising that one guest kept the silver goblet with which Grenville's men had served him.

When the Englishmen discovered after the dinner dishes were washed that one goblet was missing, they assumed—by the Elizabethan code—that it had been craftily stolen. The law of "an eye for an eye, and a tooth for a tooth" instantly prevailed. As their historian wrote, "The 16th [of July] we returned thence, and one of our boats with the Admiral [Amadas] was sent to Aquascogoc, to demand a silver cup which one of the savages had stolen from us; and not receiving it, according to his promise, we burned and spoiled their corn and town, all the people being fled." The sword had been effective; the thievery had been avenged. And Grenville had no inkling of how long a shadow his action would cast.

The English ship the *Tiger* had been laid up for repairs since it went aground in shoal waters near the present island of Portsmouth. Shipwrights had made her seaworthy again while Grenville's explorations were in progress, and the fleet turned toward Hatteras Island. Ferdinándo soon discovered an inlet through the barrier reefs close to Roanoke Island which the first expedition had explored the year before. They sailed through it and landed their men, livestock, and supplies on the north end of the island.

Now those members of the company who had been out of their element as mariners or as quiet observers of the local scene, as John White had been, took over. The blacksmith set up his forge and began to make nails. Other men dug clay which the Indians helped them find and baked bricks in the sun for foundations. Woodsmen felled trees and hewed them into posts and siding. As carpenters and masons built cottages a story and a half or two stories high, thatchers cut reeds which grew abundantly in the marshes and put the roofs in place.

Meanwhile, an earthen fort was built nearby, roughly star shaped for easier defense where marksmen could sight possible attackers not only on a direct line but at an angle. Trenches were dug inside below ground level so that earthworks of moderate height would conceal a man standing erect behind them. Raids by the Spaniards were anticipated by Raleigh's soldiers, but these preparations must have seemed ominous to the peaceful members of Wingina's tribe. Still, the chief visited the English settlement and met Grenville and the newly appointed governor of the colony, Ralph Lane. Wingina's people showed the colonists how to build fish traps, stretching nets in a huge circle around poles sunk in the coastal water, and they planted crops for them.

Among all these Elizabethan experts in crafts and in warfare, there appear to have been no farmers. If there were, they somehow were deluded into thinking their own expertise was unnecessary in this paradise. Or perhaps they were lulled into complacency by the fact that soon after they arrived at Roanoke, Captain John Arundel had sailed for England in one of the ships to expedite the sending of additional supplies to "the new fort in Virginia." By early fall all the deep draft ships in the fleet had put out, planning to make the voyage profitable by attacking Spanish ships on their way home.

As food became less abundant, Lane left one group on Roanoke and sent another south to Ocracoke; he sent a third to Hatteras where the bounty of the forests and ocean could more nearly supply their needs. From these outposts, too, it was easier for small parties to explore the nearby land and waterways.

Lane himself and one group of explorers rowed north to scout the Chowanoke territory of King Menatonon, an ally of King Wingina of Roanoke. They arrived in their four-oared boat just below Menatonon's village across the Chowan River from present-day Edenton, just as Menatonon and messengers from Wingina were conferring about the white strangers to the south. The Roanoke king was beginning to have grave doubts about the men he had welcomed so hospitably on their arrival, doubts which knowledge of the Aquascogoc affair increased.

Lane had been selected as governor partially on account of his experience in quelling rebel uprisings against the queen; without a qualm he marched directly into the Indians' meeting and put Menatonon, normally a peaceful man, under arrest. Fortunately, Lane did not draw his sword as hastily as Grenville had done earlier; for in conferring with the old chief, he learned of a great bay even farther north where pearls were plentiful and harbors deep. The Indians called it "Chesopik." Gladdened by this news, Lane soon released his prisoner and returned down river.

Winter came on, that time on the Outer Banks of little snow but of ice, piercing winds, and seas that could freeze a man sooner than they could drown him. The colony, relying on the natural abundance of game and fish, managed to survive; in spring they planted corn which by June they hoped would replenish their meager supply.

Meanwhile John White and Thomas Hariot worked feverishly to catalog the flora and fauna of the area, the lifestyle of the Indians, and the potential products the land could produce for trade. Each in his own way described the "excellent good fish," the flounder, mullet, porpoise, and shellfish; the squirrels, bears, and other edible game; and the timber suitable for building fine furniture or stout ships. Twenty-four hours in a day were scarcely enough for White who had never before had such a challenge. Quietly he would sit and watch the Indians at work or at their ceremonial dances — sketching, sketching, his pencil recording each detail. Then he would color in the outlines with a range of hues as varied as the life he saw there.

Late in May, however, the colonists had trouble with Wingina's Indians at Dasemunkepeuc, the mainland village. Grievances had mounted on both sides, and a short but bloody battle ensued. Wingina, the settlers' former friend, was killed: the peace was uneasy. This and their concern over dwindling reserves of salt, food, and ammunition made the men desperate for the arrival of the *Tiger* with supplies and the relief expedition promised by Sir Richard Grenville.

At last in June a man from the outpost on Croatoan brought word that English ships had been sighted. They proved to be Sir Francis Drake's fleet of twenty-three vessels returning from profitable raids on Florida and the Spanish West Indies. When he heard of their plight, Drake offered them several ships and enough supplies to last a month. But before the fleet sailed, a hurricane destroyed those shallow-draft ships suitable for use in the waters surrounding the island.

Ralph Lane called the 103 settlers together. "Shall we stay?" he asked them, "or shall we sail back with Drake?" Most of the men were discouraged. They had given up hope of the reinforcements promised them. The majority voted to ask Drake to take them aboard for the return voyage to England. They sailed away on June 18, 1586. Only a week later the *Tiger* arrived in the sound at the abandoned fort; in a few days more, Grenville and his three ships made port. In discouragement, Grenville left a party of fifteen men at Roanoke with two years' supplies and sailed back home.

Raleigh was not so easily turned aside from his colonial dreams. Taking into account the work White and Hariot had done and the reports of others in the party, he decided to send out another group of colonists the following year. These, however, were to settle on the shore of Chesapeake Bay where deep anchorage could be found, and, instead of being made up as a military unit, the party of 150 was to include families. Raleigh chose John White as governor. Simon Ferdinándo was again to sail as pilot.

On July 22, 1587, the first two ships arrived at Hatteras, and the third caught up with them three days later. They put in to Roanoke Island to contact the men left there by Grenville, and White led an advance party that hiked to the site of the little city. The houses were in fair shape, although vines were somewhat overgrown, and a few deer were grazing on the dirt floors. However, there was only one grim sign of the men—a skeleton bleached white in the sun. A Croatoan relative of Manteo's told White that eleven of the men had been ambushed by the Roanokes of Wingina's tribe and that the other four had put out in a boat for a small nearby island and were never seen again.

Both Ferdinándo and White were acutely aware that the hurricane season was approaching. Time to select the site for the new Chesapeake Bay colony was at a premium; nevertheless, White was stunned when the pilot refused to take them any farther. Ferdinándo told White bluntly that if he didn't get back to the main sea lanes immediately, he would lose all chance of capturing a Spanish prize. White, too, was wary of the rapid approach of cold weather and knew that crops that would mature quickly must be planted at once to last them through the winter. Also, his daughter, Eleanor Dare, and her young husband were among the colonists; both she and another of the wives, Margerie Harvie, were expecting babies

Following page:
A typical coastal forest
of scrub oaks,
scuppernong vines, and underbrush
seen at Roanoke Island.

momentarily. Consequently he reviewed Raleigh's original plans and decided to remain at Roanoke for the time being and repair the fort and houses.

A few days later, while the others were at work in the garden or cleaning out the vines and a year's windblown sand and leaves from the little houses, George Howe offered to go crabbing for their dinner. At first they could see him as he netted the big blue crustaceans, but he wandered farther and farther from the fort in hopes of an even larger catch. Near the water where Howe was crabbing, several Indians were hunting deer. Suddenly they turned on the unsuspecting Englishman, and in a matter of minutes, sixteen arrows had pierced his body. As he fell into the tall sea grass, they ran forward with vicious war cries and beat in his head with their wooden clubs. When White found him a few hours afterward, he was overcome not only with grief but rage, and no little alarm. The Croatoans again accused the Roanoke Island Indians of the murder; and White felt he had no choice but to avenge Howe's death as well as that of the eleven Englishmen whom Grenville had left there the past summer.

White planned a dawn raid on the Roanokes' village of Dasemunkepeuc. As he and twenty-four other men drew near in the half-light, White saw a group of Indians around a campfire at the center of the village. The Englishmen fired quickly, injuring one, and as the other red men fled into the swamp, the Englishmen charged after them with their sabers. Grimly, White felt he had done his duty.

Only a few hours later, he learned from Manteo that he had made a terrible blunder. The Roanokes had slipped out of their village the night before and made their silent way into the forest. The shadowy forms his men had fired on were the friendly Croatoans who had gone into the village to pick up whatever fruit and corn Wingina's tribe had left behind in its flight! White was horrified to have fired on Manteo's people, and it took all the diplomacy that his friend Manteo could muster to explain the Englishman's error to his people and to gain at least their verbal forgiveness.

The following week was a better one for John White. On August 13, he watched Manteo's baptism as a Christian and then knighted him, by order of Sir Walter Raleigh, as Lord of Roanoke and Dasemunkepeuc "in reward of his faithful service." Five days later, the governor became a grandfather. A tiny baby girl was born to Eleanor and Ananias Dare and christened Virginia as the first English child born in that country. Several days later the Harvies' baby was born. White now turned his attention to harvesting the few late summer crops.

Other supplies would soon be needed — salt for preserving, livestock, and additional food to supplement their garden crops. The ships Ferdinándo had left with them were loaded with wood and water for the return to England. Then disagreements broke out over who could best expedite the voyage and come back with supplies. The little band of settlers felt they could trust no one but their governor to go with the fleet. But White knew that the move to a new location must soon be underway, and he also felt that Raleigh would criticize his early return from his post. However, the majority prevailed, and he agreed to go. First, however, he arranged with the settlers to leave word of the location to which they moved carved on a tree,

and if they left in danger of any sort, to add a cross above the sign. Then reluctantly he sailed for England.

The voyage was harrowing—it took three storm-tossed months. As soon as Governor White arrived, Raleigh began preparations for the relief ship and a fleet with additional men and provisions to sail in the spring. White fretted restlessly through the winter.

At last Grenville received orders from the queen—but they revealed the news that a Spanish Armada was being formed to invade England. All available ships were to stand by to reinforce the fleet of Sir Francis Drake to defend England. The orders were bitterest for John White whose heart lay 3,000 impossible miles across the Atlantic. Two small, poorly equipped ships were finally allotted to him, but soon after he was allowed to sail, the ships were attacked by the French and forced to turn back to England.

The Spanish Armada was eventually defeated, but interminable delays arose before White got passage with a privateering expedition. It was late on an August evening in 1590 when the ships anchored at last off Hatteras. White's eager eyes could see smoke rising in the direction of Roanoke Island. Though he was surprised that his colony had not moved its location as planned, he was overjoyed to picture the colonists resting after their day's work as he had done on that same shore.

Early the next morning two boats were lowered into rough and angry waters, and the men set out for Nags Head where a second column of smoke could be seen. But it was only a woods fire, and the next day they put out again, this time to Roanoke. As they crossed the sound in swelling waves, one boat capsized and six men and their captain drowned. In their grief and anxiety, White and his party overshot the location of the fort and had to anchor in the sound overnight opposite a point from which they saw a light shining through the trees.

John White recorded the daily life of the Roanoke Island Indians in realistic paintings while Thomas Hariot described them. Indian village and artifacts photographed at Roanoke Island Historical Park.

White and Hariot, each in his own way, recorded the summertime of the islands of the Outer Banks, its flowers and wildlife.

"We sounded with a trumpet a call, and afterwards [played] many English tunes of songs, and called to them friendly; but we had no answer," he recalled. At daybreak he eagerly helped row ashore and hurried toward the fort. As they drew near, the forest was strangely silent. On a tree as they approached, they discovered three letters had been carved: CRO. There were the prints of bare feet in the sand, and a rotten tree was smouldering, but that was all.

In frantic haste, White led the way through the woods to where the first expedition had built their houses—those same sturdy little cottages which the Dares, the Harvies, the Viccars, and the Archards had repaired and moved into. When he reached the clearing, he stopped and stared. The area had been enclosed with a tall palisade of trees, but the houses themselves had been taken down—not burned, not destroyed—they had simply vanished! Suddenly one of his men shouted that he had discovered another message. Near the entrance, the bark had been peeled from a tree and the name CROATOAN had been carved on it. White ran to examine it. Was there a Maltese cross—the danger sign—carved above it? No, only the one word appeared. Thank God for that!

Croatoan was the island on which Manteo had been born; it was the name of the tribe which so often had been the Englishmen's friend. If the colonists had indeed moved to Croatoan, perhaps they were safe there. At the fort, overgrown with grass and melon vines, White found bars and pieces of metal, guns, and a few other objects which, he reasoned, might have been too heavy for them to carry. All was not lost. Perhaps by tomorrow they would be reunited at Croatoan.

Now another storm was brewing. The tall sea grass was bending over under the wind, and the light was growing milky. The men hurried to the shore and rowed back to their ship as quickly as possible. A storm off Hatteras blew them out to sea. As the ship plowed forward, leaving the Outer Banks farther and farther astern, White's cheeks were wet with more than the salt spray that coated his lips, stung his eyes, and drenched his clothing. How powerless is man against the elements! The powerful seas and a treacherous gale blew them toward the Azores; from there they steered a limping course to England. It was October 1590. His granddaughter, Virginia Dare, was three years and two months old if she still lived, and John White was older than any man had a right to be

Following page: Near Manteo, along the coast of Roanoke Sound, a weather-bleached skiff lies abandoned in the tall marsh grass.

When John White returned to his colony in 1590 he found only bars of iron, guns, and other objects too heavy to carry easily, scattered near the fort—by then overgrown with grass and vines. From the diorama at Fort Raleigh National Historic Site.

as he walked down the gangway to Plymouth. He would soon learn that Raleigh had fallen from the queen's favor. Where could a poor painter, governor for one short month of active duty, ever in this world raise the money to sail again to rejoin his royal colony?

Not until 1608 was the fate of the colony determined, and even that was hypothesis. When Captain John Smith sent men out from his Jamestown colony to explore the region south of the James, they brought back word from Indians that there were people living among the Chowanokes, those friendly allies of the Croatoan, who lived in houses similar to those of the English, who wore clothes, and who owned much brass. Others reported that most of the white families from Roanoke had been slaughtered in an attack by Powhatan's tribe after it had been warned by its medicine men that a new colony would arise on the Chesapeake that would "give end to his Empire." Seven of the whites—four men, two boys, and one young maiden—had escaped to the Chowanoke territory. A few years later, as such reports continued to filter into Jamestown, the community's historian Samuel Purchase wrote: "Powhatan confessed to Captain Smith that he had been at their slaughter [all but those seven], and had divers utensils of theirs to shew."

When night fell over the English coast of the Atlantic, old John White could look westward across the water in the sun's last rays and dream that Manteo's people had taken in the remnants of his little band, his "lost colony," and that the land he had painted so lovingly had sheltered them.

For decades the vast land of Carolina lay almost as undisturbed by white men as it was before John White arrived in 1584. With only a vague impression of the territory, King Charles I in 1629 made a handsome present of it to his attorney general, Sir Robert Heath. Its boundaries were defined as the Atlantic on the east to the South Seas on the west, and from the southern shore of Albemarle Sound to a few miles north of the present state of Florida. Charles I gave Heath a great deal of power in ruling the land but ordered the new proprietor to keep a twenty-ounce gold crown in Carolana, as he named the region, for the king's use when making a state visit to the New World. Unfortunately, King Charles lost his head before it could wear the Carolana crown.

Little came of Heath's proprietorship, partly because of the civil war that erupted in England. From 1649 to 1660, while Oliver Cromwell guided the affairs of the Commonwealth, Carolana was not a primary concern to the mother country. Meanwhile, a few settlers moved down from Virginia and purchased land from the Indians. Nathaniel Batts built a house on the Roanoke River in the 1650s as did Samuel Pricklove and George Durant.

Across the Atlantic, King Charles II was returned to his father's throne in 1660, after Cromwell's rule came to an end. The king was deep in debt to the Royalists who had supported him. Money was scarce, but colonial land was plentiful, and eight of his contributors suggested that they would consider themselves amply repaid if the king would make them "the true and absolute Lords and Proprietaries" over the territory his lately beheaded

father had granted to Sir Robert Heath. The king did even better. He enlarged the territory—now called the Province of Carolina—to the southern border of Virginia and south below the old Spanish city of St. Augustine.

He issued a charter for the province that was extremely liberal in many respects. It contained such generous provisions as freedom of religion, the right to be tried only within Carolina, England, or Wales, and it guaranteed settlers the same rights as free-born Englishmen.

The eight proprietors included Edward Hyde, Earl of Clarendon; George Monck, Duke of Albemarle; William, Earl of Craven; Lord John Berkeley; Anthony Ashley-Cooper; Sir George Carteret; Sir John Colleton; and Sir William Berkeley, governor of Virginia and brother of John. Their primary interest was to make a successful business venture of the ownership of these colonial lands. The immediate necessity was to promote settlement and

the production of marketable goods there, for the population of North Carolina was only about 500. A great promotion and advertising campaign began.

The Albemarle region in the north was the first to develop. Its early citizens such as Batts, Pricklove, and Durant had little interest in the new government and less enthusiasm for the new restrictions on their trade. They were particularly annoyed by the grants issued by their neighbor, Governor Berkeley of Virginia. He ignored their land purchases from the Indians and even granted Durant's land, on which he was well established, to George Catchmaid, bringing on lengthy litigation.

Life had proceeded in the region with harmony between the settlers and the Indians and without governmental interference. For decades to come, this determined independence of the men of Perquimans (as the precinct was named) led to dissension with the Lords Proprietors. By 1665 in spite of an unenthusiastic reception, proprietary government was an

accepted fact with the people of Albemarle—about fifty families in the precinct of Perquimans alone—having their own governor, council, and assembly. In 1669 the proprietors began to fear they were building up "a numerous Democracy" and issued a new constitution written by John Locke. It emphasized the feudal powers of the Lords Proprietors, including the granting of titles of nobility, and greatly restrained what power the people exercised. This was only the first revision, but the total effect of these and later changes might be stated very simply: they perpetuated a state of confusion and conflict between the officials and the people that in varying degrees lasted throughout the sixty-six years of the proprietorship, with no legal avenues open to settle grievances.

By the beginning of the eighteenth century, a certain amount of progress had been achieved in spite of political unrest, and the population began to center around the future town sites of Edenton, Bath, and New Bern. In 1700, John Lawson, a young college graduate

from Yorkshire, England, sailed for Charleston, South Carolina, after reading one of the Lords Proprietors' promotional tracts. With several English friends and an Indian guide Lawson set out to explore the North Carolina back country. He was particularly fascinated by the Indians, for he found in them a physical perfection which he greatly admired and highly developed skills to meet the challenges of their environment. "I have known some of them very strong," he marveled, "and as for running and leaping, they are extraordinary fellows, and will dance for several nights together with the greatest briskness imaginable, their wind never failing them."

Lawson did not find them faultless, however, and observed that once they tasted a little rum they wanted to get completely drunk. And he remarked prophetically, as he observed the relationships of various tribes, "The Indians are very revengeful and never forget an injury done till they have received satisfaction." However, the farther he traveled, the more he felt that compared to the crowded villages of England this spacious land was paradise.

Lawson and his friends turned back to the coast by a more northerly route than they had taken on their trip out, sometimes hiking, sometimes paddling canoes. There the young student began to find settlements of English families. The men, he observed, were "commonly of a bashful, sober behavior," hard to get to know, but the women—ah! they were "well featured, with very brisk, charming eyes which sets them off to advantage." They married young, he noted somewhat wistfully, and he was impressed that these desirable creatures were also "very handy in canoes and [would] manage them with great dexterity and skill, which they become accustomed to in this watery country." They could also weave cloth

Surveyor John Lawson explored the back country in 1701 *(pages 28-29)* and recorded his impressions of the Piedmont area in his journal.

from flax and cotton that they grew, in addition to performing their usual household chores.

By the time he reached the plantation home of Richard Smith on the Pamlico River, he had decided he could never return to the structured life of England. Here in the new precinct of Bath he concluded (as the Lords Proprietors had already done) that with the convenient nearby location of Ocracoke Inlet, a town could become a profitable port. Together with Joel Martin Sr., and Simon Alderson, he purchased a choice piece of property on the quiet waters of a sheltered bay on the Pamlico River. Soon he dusted off his surveying instruments and began to lay out a town to be known as Bath. It would contain lots for houses, as well as a town common, and a site for a church and glebe for St. Thomas Parish of the Church of England. The whole village would be enclosed by a fence to keep out wild animals. By 1705 (or 1706 — the date is uncertain) Bath was incorporated as the first town in the province of North Carolina. By 1708 it had approximately fifty to sixty residents, and its lot-holders included a doctor, Maurice Leullyn; a future chief justice, Christopher Gale; and the governor, Thomas Cary.

Soon life in the new town took on a different aspect. Sloops from other colonies, and even an occasional ship from England, came into port. Boats from inland plantations anchored in the bay, riding low in the water when they arrived with their produce, riding high after their owners struck a bargain with a local merchant and delivered their cargo. Merchants opened shops on the ground floors of their frame houses; Lawson, Leullyn, and Major Gale operated a horse mill on Water Street for grinding grain; church services were held on Sunday mornings in Gale's parlor where a young lawyer read a prayer and sermon.

Although Lawson could hear wolves and panthers howling at night, the animals rarely ventured beyond the town fence. He worried, though, about keeping the friendship of the Indians and constantly told his neighbors, "They are really better to us than we are to them." While the Indians traded on the town streets, he could at least exercise some authority to see that they were properly treated. He was disturbed that some Indian children had been stolen and enslaved on the pretense of bringing them up as Christians, and certain merchants had a peculiar notion that it was a Christian action to charge the Indians more than they did white settlers.

In 1708 Lawson finished writing a book on his exploration of the province and sailed for London to confer with possible publishers. Here he met with some of the Lords Proprietors and was made surveyor-general of the colony. This added to his interest in meeting another London visitor Baron Christoph von Graffenried, a member of a Swiss company interested in settling Swiss and German immigrants in the New World. The Lords Proprietors gave him a bargain rate; Lawson added his glowing descriptions of the colony, and the baron shortly decided to buy a large tract there.

The first group of Swiss settlers sailed for Carolina with Lawson in January, and von Graffenried followed in July with an additional group. Lawson surveyed the new town, which the baron named Neuse-Bern for the river which bordered it and the Swiss town from which he came. It was laid out in the shape of a cross for religious significance and also for reasons of

Lawson was attracted by the talented young women he met in the frontier settlements and wrote of their ability to weave cloth from their own cotton and flax. Photograph at left from the Polk Farm, Pineville.

defense. The Indians were alarmed at this further encroachment on their hunting grounds and even more so as settlers began confiscating the muskets of any Indian who ventured close. A situation which had long been uneasy grew rapidly worse. Perhaps, with hindsight, it was less the effect of any particular action between Indians and white landholders that suddenly overwhelmed the Pamlico area than the fact that two unalterable and contradictory ways of life met head on and found no way to compromise.

Bath and its neighbor New Bern (which the town soon came to be called) were caught in a series of crises that summer of 1711. Deadly yellow fever touched almost every home and drought wiped out crops.

John Lawson, involved with a surveyor's concerns—how far upriver the Neuse was navigable and the distance from the coast to the mountains—organized a boat trip to explore the river with Christopher Gale and von Graffenried. At the last moment, Gale's family came down with yellow fever, but Lawson and the Swiss baron decided to go on. They left on an early September morning and to Lawson's astonishment were captured a few days later by sixty armed Indians who carried them to King Hancock at the Tuscarora town of Catechna. It was all a mistake, Lawson reasoned, for these were his friends, all of them. He seemed to be right when Hancock called a council meeting that night and decided to release them.

But the next morning, as the two white men were climbing into their canoes, a new contingent of Indians arrived including Cor Tom, a chief from Core Banks whom Lawson considered a troublemaker. Cor Tom demanded the right to question them; Lawson, his nerves stretched to razor edge by this unjustified treatment, let loose an angry outburst against him. Blood, they say, is thicker than water—Indian blood being no exception. The next morning another council of chiefs was called, and when it ended, von Graffenried was a temporary prisoner. John Lawson, by means of one of the blood-curdling rites he had described in his book, was on his way to a slow and painful death. An Indian, he had said, will not rest until the wrong done to him is avenged.

On September 27, war parties under King Hancock slipped into the forest surrounding Bath, New Bern, and the isolated farms of Pamticough County, and a few hours later the autumn air was filled with hideous warcries as 500 warriors committed atrocities on more than 140 white women, men, and children that even today turn the blood cold. Thirty unfortunate victims were captured and tortured.

It took four grim years of unbelievable cruelty on both sides, of near starvation, and of fear—all the horror called the Tuscarora Wars—before peace returned to John Lawson's town, von Graffenried's larger settlement, and the plantations in the land around them. When the wars ended, the Indians had been defeated but at great cost. The treaty that was signed agreed "that there be a firm, perpetual and inviolable peace to continue as long as the sun and moon endure between all and every inhabitant and people of North Carolina and all the people of the Tuscarora Indians."

32   The Jordan House in Bertie County, near Windsor, was built about 1713, its brick laid in Flemish bond with glazed headers.

Begun in 1734, St. Thomas Church at Bath, the oldest town in North Carolina, is the oldest church in continuous use in the state. Many victims of the Tuscarora Wars are buried under the tile floor of the sanctuary.

John Lawson and Thomas Cary were gone and so was Baron von Graffenried, who had mortgaged war ravaged New Bern to Thomas Pollock and returned in sorrow to Switzerland. However, Bath had several new distinguished citizens when peace returned to the Pamlico area. One was Governor Charles Eden, who purchased a town house and two lots on Bay Street. Another settled in the county nearby, Eden's secretary and acting chief justice, Tobias Knight.

Meanwhile, another newcomer's house is said to have gone up on Plum's Point; its owner, an extremely wealthy merchant, introduced himself to his new neighbors as Edward Teach. He was an outsize, muscular, handsome man and reportedly gave marvelous parties to which the colonial and town officials and their families journeyed in keen anticipation.

Teach's career had moved rapidly from that of merchant seaman in Queen Anne's War, to privateer out of Jamaica, to buccaneer under Captain Benjamin Hornygold who put Teach in command of a captured French merchantman in the summer of 1717. Hornygold and his new captain sailed into the Bahamas where they heard a juicy tidbit at the first tavern they entered. King George I had offered amnesty to any pirate who took an oath of loyalty to the Crown. For Hornygold—middle-aged, wealthy, and weary—this offer had great appeal. He made his way posthaste to the office of the new governor Woodes Rogers, who had vowed to wipe out piracy, and promised to reform. He urged Teach to do likewise.

What nonsense this appeared to a giant of a man in the prime of his life, a man purported to have twelve wives in twelve different ports, who found it both joyous and judicious to keep sailing! Besides, he had just become master of his first ship which was currently being mounted with forty guns. He rechristened her the *Queen Anne's Revenge*, rounded up a crew long on daring and short on scruples, and put out to sea. Teach had served a valuable apprenticeship under Captain Hornygold, and by eagerly applying himself to his trade, he soon became even more infamous than his master.

Teach was a forgettable name, so he quickly changed it to Blackbeard. The name suited a man whose whiskers, if such they could be tamely called, rippled black as jet from below his eyes to his rib cage. Across his chest he wore a sash or sling which held three pairs of deadly pistols within the flick of his finger.

Like most pirates, Blackbeard knew that winning a merchant prize by gunfire was far riskier than accepting her surrender the minute he bellowed, "Heave to." Consequently, in every port he entered, he spread ferocious, bloody tales about himself—some true. He braided his beard and tied the pigtails with ribbons, and just as he approached a hapless ship, he would light two of the slow-burning matches used to touch off the cannon and stick the ends under his hat so that sulphurous smoke seemed to pour out of each ear. The combined effect of plundering, gossip, and showmanship soon won for him a reputation second to none among buccaneers. One sight of him and another cargo was on its way to the hold of *Queen Anne's Revenge;* one more ship was burned and its crew set adrift in boats.

In the Bay of Honduras, Blackbeard came across another *Revenge* whose captain was

When the Chowan River was wrapped in fog, a pirate such as Blackbeard could sail his ship silently into a cove and hide among the cypress trees.

Major Stede Bonnet, known as "the gentleman pirate." Bonnet's air of class appealed to Blackbeard, and he suggested they join forces. Not many days out from port on the way up the Carolina coast, Blackbeard noted that his new friend lacked all but the bare rudiments of seamanship, a disconcerting trait in a seagoing partner. With unaccustomed diplomacy, he soon persuaded Bonnet to lead a life of gentlemanly leisure aboard Blackbeard's own ship while letting a lieutenant take over the irksome duties of the helm of Bonnet's vessel. Thus reorganized, the two *Revenges* looted at least twelve well-stocked merchantmen that season and enlarged their own numbers to a flotilla of four. Now Blackbeard's only problem was how to take the lion's share for himself and still live to enjoy it.

At Topsail Inlet, not far north of Cape Fear, he found his opportunity. Running the two smaller ships aground, he generously offered Bonnet command again of his own ship and relayed the news that King George had extended his Act of Grace to pirates for another year. He personally was going to take advantage of this, he told Bonnet, and urged the major to go to Bath and take the oath himself. Anticipating a division of the rich rewards of their labor, Bonnet heeded his advice and took off at once to see Governor Eden. The governor not only granted him the king's pardon but gave him permission to set sail for St. Thomas. There, the governor said, a man of his talents could quickly obtain letters of Marque and Reprisal to sail as a privateer in England's service.

The delighted Bonnet hurried back to take command of his ship and set his course for the West Indies. But at Topsail he discovered that Blackbeard, his favored friends, and all the booty had sailed away! Bonnet rounded up the loyal crew members who had been marooned on an island and set out in pursuit to Ocracoke where they said Blackbeard was headed. Their paths never crossed again. Bonnet, infuriated and no longer rich, returned to piracy.

Blackbeard, meanwhile, made his way to Bath and to a warm welcome from the governor. There, basking in the friendship of Eden and Tobias Knight, Blackbeard settled down to the respectable life, took a winsome new wife of sixteen years, and reportedly built his house on Plum's Point.

With the influx of Blackbeard's cronies, Bath enjoyed the sudden prosperity of a town to which a new industry has suddenly been added. Shopkeepers did a booming business, taverns were filled, and money flowed freely. When life became a little dull for Squire Teach, he would take a business trip to the pleasant island of Ocracoke and return with a wide variety of luxurious custom-free merchandise to sell. One time he even sailed up the Pamlico with a handsome French Guineaman, loaded to the gunwales with casks of rum, sugar, cocoa, and spices. He had, he told Governor Eden, found her drifting aimlessly in the Atlantic, her crew having apparently abandoned ship. "Possibly in a storm—you know how rough it gets off Hatteras."

The governor convened an extralegal Admiralty Court presided over by loyal Tobias Knight; the court called her a "legitimate prize" and gave Mr. Teach the right to sell her cargo. Teach naturally sent a gift to Governor Eden and Justice Knight—sixty hogsheads of

Following page: The wreck of the *Laura S. Barnes* on Bodie Island in the Outer Banks (*inset*) is only one of hundreds of ships that met their end in the treacherous storms off Hatteras.

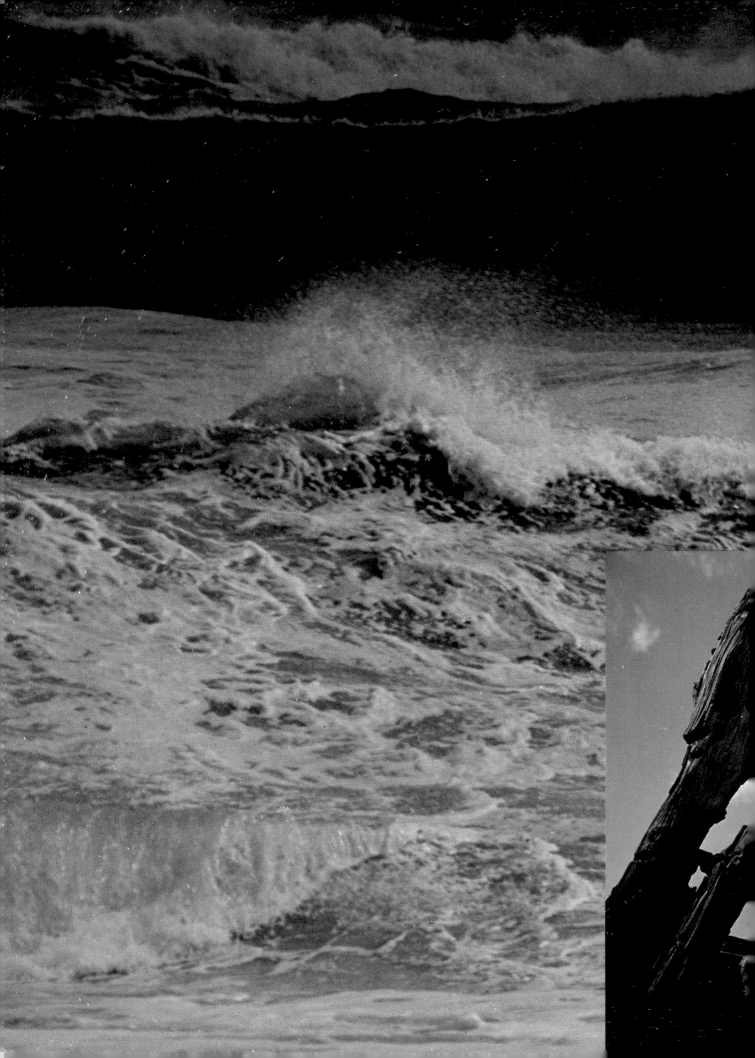

At Teach's Hole, Lieutenant Robert Maynard attacked Blackbeard and his crew. The pirates were killed or captured, but some say Blackbeard's headless body swam around the ship seven times before sinking.

sugar to the governor and twenty to his secretary, although unfriendly gossip called this the cut they demanded.

Among those who refused to accept the respectability of Bath's new citizen was Governor Alexander Spotswood of Virginia. His colony's trade had been seriously disrupted by pirates who darted from the Outer Banks to overtake the traders who normally sailed in and out of Virginia ports. In November 1718, Governor Spotswood swung into action. He engaged two sloops, armed them heavily, and manned them with sailors from two British men-of-war. Then he dispatched them to Carolina under the command of Lieutenant Robert Maynard.

Blackbeard in his ship *Adventure* was lying at anchor in Teach's Hole, his favorite bay at Ocracoke. Here he received the disturbing news in a veiled note from Tobias Knight. Blackbeard was undaunted. He threw a party, a wholesome way to spend an evening, breathing in the invigorating salt air of the island and singing a few chanties to beguile his fisherman friends on shore. As the moon sank into Teach's Hole, one of his lieutenants, apparently not quite so confident of the morrow's outcome, ventured a question.

"Cap'n," he said, "not to be personal, but does yer young wife know where yer treasure's hid?"

Blackbeard threw back his enormous head and laughed uproariously. Then he lurched forward, mug in hand, and let loose a string of oaths that would have sizzled the ears of Lieutenant Maynard, anchored just beyond the cove.

"Nobody knows but m'self and the devil," he bellowed. "And may the longest liver take all!"

As dawn broke, wrapping the island in silver as it often does over the Outer Banks before the red sun breaks through, Maynard weighed anchor on the *Ranger* and sailed within hailing distance. Blackbeard leaped to the top of the cabin and shouted a profane greeting.

"Villains!" he boomed. "From whence come you?"

For reply Maynard ordered the British ensign to be run up and emphasized his action by shouting, "You can see by our colors we're not pirates!"

"Send over a boat, if you dare, so I can see for myself who you are."

"I can't spare a boat, but I'll come aboard myself with my sloop as soon as I can," sneered the lieutenant.

"Damnation seize my soul if I give you quarter or take any from you!" The pirate shook his fist in the direction of the British sloop. With this he gave a quick command to hoist sail, slash the anchor cable, and run up his own black flag with its white skull and crossbones. The battle was on.

The fight was long, and it was bitter. Ten of Maynard's men and nine of Blackbeard's lay dead in pools of blood that dripped from the decks into the tranquil bay.

At last it was the pirate and the navy man in hand to hand combat. Both men fired their pistols at close range, but Blackbeard's missed and Maynard's struck home. Still the pirate fought on, his razor-sharp cutlass breaking the Britisher's weapon as though it were a child's toy. As he raised his arm to strike the final blow, one of Maynard's sailors swung around, sword in hand, and slashed the pirate's throat. Choking, Blackbeard pulled another pistol from his sling and fell dead as he was still cocking it. He had fought to outlive the devil through twenty slashes of the cutlass and five pistol balls.

The triumphant Lieutenant Maynard hacked off the pirate's head and hung it from his bowsprit. Then he weighed anchor and sailed for Bath. He made his way up the Pamlico River at dusk and anchored at a pier along Water Street, the grisly head of Bath's patron looming through the dark like a bloody trophy.

There were few smiles on the faces of Bath's citizens and no cheering reception. Mr. Teach may not have been altogether on the up-and-up, they reasoned, but then he wasn't all bad either. The Outer Bankers at Ocracoke took much the same attitude. He'd brought many a fine piece of merchandise to their shore at reasonable prices, and no one favored the king's custom duties. At least he was aboveboard in his villainy and cheated them less than the overbearing Portsmouth merchants.

None of Blackbeard's redeeming features was noticeable to the coastal traders who had trembled when they saw his ensign flying nor to the Virginians whose port activities had slowed to a halt. Nor were they appreciated by Governor Spotswood when his sloops returned with pirate loot discovered under the hay in Tobias Knight's barn and with the incriminating letter from the chief justice found in Blackbeard's cabin. Maurice Moore, Edward Mosely, and Jeremiah Vail, members of the General Assembly who had doggedly tracked down evidence to bring Knight to trial and were consequently arrested for "interference," had no regrets.

The Governor's Council, after hearing the case, declared Knight "a good and faithful officer," not guilty of conspiracy with the pirate, but the three assemblymen were convicted and fined. Governor Eden declared that Spotswood had illegally invaded North Carolina waters and refused to admit any embroilment in illegal activities. Disregarding him, the Virginia courts tried and hanged Blackbeard's crew in Williamsburg. As for his treasure, "the Devil (who was 'the longest liver') may have taken it."

North Carolina was no longer a haven for pirates; peaceful merchants could once more sail along her coast, subject only to the greater dangers of shoals, high seas, and hurricanes. The Golden Age of Piracy had ended.

As piracy faded into legend, North Carolina trade showed a healthy increase. From all along Albemarle Sound, sloops and schooners were loaded with barrels of salt pork, tar or pitch, Indian corn, and occasional baskets of peas and beans, cheese, bundles of hides, or boxes of beeswax. The ships took the ocean route through Currituck Inlet north to Norfolk, Virginia. Here, with many complaints about the low prices received and the high prices charged, the skipper fortified himself at a waterfront tavern and then loaded his cargo for the return voyage. Casks of Jamaica rum were taken aboard as were hogsheads of molasses and packages of English goods that found an eager market in Carolina. Here, where farms were carved from forests or thick tangles of riverside underbrush, tools were in great demand—hatchets, hoes, axes and nails, muskets and powder; and household goods such as kettles and waffle irons, fine fabrics, buttons, buckles, and ribbon.

Trade also flowed along new roads—mere cart tracks that were "mudholes in wet weather and dust bowls in dry." These roads ran along either side of the Great Dismal Swamp to Kempsville and Great Bridge in Virginia from "ye town on Queen Anne's Creek" which in 1722 was named Edenton; along them, Albemarle farmers drove their cattle, hogs, and horses to market.

As the first town in the most populous section of the colony, Edenton grew rapidly. In 1718 it already had a frame courthouse and a public landing, and ten years later it boasted fifty small frame houses along its wide tree-lined streets that ran down to Edenton Bay in the

Chowan River. It also had one truly splendid mansion on the corner of Broad and Water streets built in 1725 by Richard Sanderson. Designed in the Jacobean style of architecture, it had a cupola from which Sanderson could watch ships come and go on the river, and it became known as the Cupola House.

For all Edenton's urbanity (it even had a law forbidding hogs from running loose in the streets), not all early visitors were impressed. Aristocratic William Byrd, the "Black Swan of Westover," a member of the commission to survey the boundary line between Virginia and North Carolina, arrived at a nearby plantation in 1728.

Colonel Byrd was a gentleman by birth and thus was relieved of the need for physical labor, but he hated idleness with such a passion that he allowed himself none among his daily exercises ("doing my dance"), scientific observations and study, overseeing his plantation, his duties in colonial government, and—not the least time-consuming—his numerous love

Preceding page:
Legends surround the ponies of the Outer Banks,
said to be descendants of horses that swam ashore from
wrecked Spanish or English ships.

affairs. Consequently, he could not comprehend the life of the Carolinians he observed.

"Surely there is no place in the world," he confided in his journal with great disdain, "where the inhabitants live with less labor than in North Carolina. It approaches nearer to the description of Lubberland [a paradise for idlers] than any other, by the great felicity of the climate, the easiness of raising provisions, and the slothfulness of the people.

"Indian corn is of so great increase that a little pain will subsist a very large family with bread, and then they may have meat without any pains at all, by the help of low grounds, and the great variety of [forage] that grows on the high land. The men for their part, just like the Indians, impose all the work upon the poor women. They make their wives rise out of their beds early in the morning, at the same time that they lie and snore till the sun has run one-third of his course and dispersed all the unwholesome damps. Then, after stretching and yawning for half an hour, they light their pipes, and, under the protection of a cloud of smoke, venture out into the open air; though, if it happens to be ever so little cold, they quickly return shivering into the chimney corner. When the weather is mild, they stand leaning with both arms upon the cornfield fence, and gravely consider whether they had best go and take a small heat at the hoe: but generally find reasons to put it off till another time.

"Thus they loiter away their lives, like Solomon's sluggard, with their arms across, and at the winding up of the year scarcely have bread to eat.

"To speak the truth, 'tis a thorough aversion to labor that makes people file off to North Carolina, where plenty and warm sun confirm them in their disposition to laziness for their whole lives."

Possibly Edenton was as happy to see Colonel Byrd leave as he was to go.

Another gentleman had left Edenton, somewhat precipitately, not long before. He was Cornelius Harnett, Sr. In 1724 when George Burrington sailed into Edenton from Devon to be sworn in as the new governor of the colony (Charles Eden having died two years previously), Harnett soon became his friend and supporter. The hot-tempered Burrington had few of either, and in fact quickly made an enemy of Chief Justice Christopher Gale (Byrd called Gale "Judge Jumble"). According to Judge Gale, Burrington threatened him almost as soon as he got off the boat, saying he would "slit his nose, crop his ears, and lay him in irons." Gale eventually sailed for England to report the governor's conduct to the Lords Proprietors, and shortly thereafter they appointed Sir Richard Everard to replace him.

Burrington's friends (Harnett among them) did not take kindly to this, and they joined the angry Devonshire man when he marched up to Everard's house and loudly demanded, "I want satisfaction of you; therefore come out and give it to me."

Sir Richard declined to do so, and Burrington "proceeded to vent wrath in a diversified and well-chosen collection of profanity, among other things characterizing him as a calf's head, a noodle, and an ape, who was no more fit to be governor than Sancho Panza!" Everard considered this noisy delegation a threat to break into his house, and he brought the matter to the attention of the attorney general. Indictments were returned against Burrington and

Harnett, and shortly afterward they made their separate ways out of Edenton. The cases were eventually filed as *nol-pros (nolle prosequi)*.

Harnett, his wife, and small son, Cornelius, Jr., made their way south to Cape Fear where they had heard that land was being opened up for the settlement of a new town. Colonel Maurice Moore, who had fought with other South Carolina troops under his brother, James, in the Tuscarora Wars, was so excited by the prospects of this unsettled region that he had stayed to explore it. In 1725 Moore obtained a large land grant there and soon laid out the town of Brunswick on a point of land twelve miles up from the river's mouth. Cornelius Harnett, Sr., bought the first two lots.

Moore was not alone in his venture. With him from Goose Creek, South Carolina, came members of "The Family" — his brother, "King" Roger Moore, and Eleazor Allen among them. At Goose Creek, The Family — closely tied by blood and marriage — had owned and operated a thriving business in the production of naval stores and proposed to do so again in the new settlement.

They were soon joined by other adventurous leaders from older parts of the colony who seemed to marry or to be adopted into The Family as quickly as they moved into town. Among them were John Baptista Ashe and his wife, Elizabeth, who came from Bath with their three children, John, Samuel, and Mary; Edward and Ann Moseley; Jeremiah Vail; and John and Samuel Swann.

Harnett opened a Publick House and operated a ferry, called the Haulover; and young Cornelius, Jr., played marbles under the live oak trees, went fishing along the banks of the river, played Indian with his bow and arrows, and learned to write his ABC's on his small slate. Harnett's erstwhile friend Burrington was furious about his new allegiance to The Family, whom Burrington considered enemies. Burrington was particularly hostile toward them after clashing with John Baptista Ashe about the ownership of two horses Burrington claimed had been stolen from him. In true form, Burrington called Harnett a "fool, blackguard, puppy!" But Harnett had chosen The Family as friends and abided by his choice. The vigor of The Family matched their enthusiasm for the land, and Brunswick soon became one of the leading ports of the colony.

In London the Board of Trade had become extremely skeptical of the quality of administration being given to the Carolina colonies by the Lords Proprietors, not unreasonably considering that six of their appointed governors had been run out of office by the citizenry. Finally they requested the proprietors of North Carolina to sell their land back to the Crown and make it a royal colony as South Carolina had been since 1719. In 1729 all but one of them agreed to do so. John Carteret, Lord Granville, refused; perhaps because he was a favorite with the reigning House of Hanover, he was allowed to keep the land grant rights to his share. The Granville District comprised the wealthiest and most heavily settled portion of the colony, extending from the Virginia line south to the middle of North Carolina. The partiality accorded Granville was to create constant problems.

Although Christopher Gale tried to prevent the Privy Council from naming Burrington as the first royal governor, the Duke of Newcastle prevailed upon them to do so. Some doubted that the new government would be any improvement over the Lords Proprietors. However, before his inflammable temper was again his undoing, Burrington managed to accomplish a surprising amount in North Carolina. He personally laid out a desperately needed highway from the Virginia line to the Cape Fear with only the assistance of Indian guides and a few surveyors; he was largely responsible for the development of the Cape Fear region, personally marking the channel of that river and Topsail Inlet; he also instigated the building of a major road linking this southern region with New Bern. These improvements were essential as the population of the colony had increased to 36,000.

When Burrington's violent conflict with The Family, the attorney general, and members of the Governor's Council were too much for even him to endure, he requested the Lords of Trade to recall him. They were greatly relieved to do so, and appointed Gabriel Johnston, an able Scotsman, to take his place in 1734. Johnston, born in 1699 at Annandale and graduated from St. Andrews University near Dundee, went to London as a political writer early in his career. However, too poor at the time of his appointment to pay his passage to America, he had to borrow money to sail to Brunswick.

Beset by many of the same problems that had plagued Burrington, Johnston had both the disposition and diplomacy to handle them, and the colony expanded under his long term of office. No more a friend of The Family than his predecessor, he soon threw his considerable weight behind the development of Newton (or New Town) which had been settled fifteen miles up the Cape Fear as a port of entry rivaling Brunswick. He renamed it Wilmington for his patron, Spencer Compton, the Earl of Wilmington.

Some progressive developments took place; other developments took one step forward and two back. The General Assembly, meeting at New Bern in 1749, passed "an act for the encouragement of James Davis, to set up and carry on his business of printer in the Province." This Mr. Davis did, arriving in New Bern shortly with his type chases, page forms, and printing press, and two years later he began publishing *The North Carolina Gazette*, the first newspaper in the colony.

Less positive was the attempt to "fix a place for the Seat of Government and for keeping public offices" and a controversy over the number of delegates from the Albemarle region. These issues became entangled when Governor Johnston asked the Assembly in 1746 to place a permanent capital at New Bern. The Albemarle delegates defeated his bill, but Johnston called a rump assembly a few months later which adopted the bill in the absence of its opponents. Incensed by this coup, the Albemarle counties refused to send delegates to the Assembly from 1746 until 1754 when the Privy Council in England finally ruled on the issue. It upheld the Albemarle point of view, allowing the older counties five representatives each to two each from the newer counties. As a result, the "itinerant capital" continued, with the state records bouncing from place to place in an ox cart!

Begun in 1727, Orton Plantation near Wilmington is resplendent each spring when millions of azaleas bloom there. Here the tomb of its founder "King" Roger Moore is shaded by Spanish moss.

Facing page: Memorabilia of three governors span North Carolina's early history, photographed in the library of Hayes Plantation at Edenton. *Below — top row, left and center:* The Palmer Marsh House in Bath; the parlor where the General Assembly met in 1744 and 1752. *Right:* Ship captains sighted the channel over the bar into Core Sound by lining up with the Hammock House in Beaufort, built around 1699. *Bottom row, left:* Parlor of Joseph Bell House in Beaufort, built around 1767. *Center:* View down Front Street in Beaufort showing the John Easton House. *Right:* Milford, built in 1746 in Camden County.

During Johnston's administration, a wave of immigration flooded the colony—from Wales, Scotland, Ireland, and Germany. Many came down the Shenandoah Valley from Pennsylvania and Virginia or across the long Wagon Road from Philadelphia into Carolina's Piedmont. The frontier was pushed farther and farther westward. Each family came for slightly different reasons, yet they were united in a single desire for new, rich land and the opportunity to begin a better life for themselves.

To entice immigrants from his homeland, Johnston offered a special inducement, with the Assembly's approval, of exempting the new settlers from public taxes for ten years. The Highland Scots sailed directly across the Atlantic to the Cape Fear. Landing at Brunswick, some settled along the coast but more moved upriver. They located their families closely enough to share their love of skirling bagpipes and the excitement of Scottish games and to chat with one another in the Gaelic tongue when the long day was over. Within a few decades their principal settlements had been incorporated as Campbelltown and Cross Creek (present-day Fayetteville). The Scotch-Irish (actually Lowland Scots who had first settled in Ulster) came down from Pennsylvania as did the Germans.

Among the Germans who sought land in Carolina were the Moravians, a Protestant sect called the United Brethren who followed the simple ways of the first Christians. Their leader was a remarkable man, Bishop Gottlieb Spangenburg, who preferred to be known as Brother Joseph. He had moved an earlier colony from Georgia, where its members had been ordered to bear arms contrary to their religious beliefs, and had settled the town of Bethlehem, Pennsylvania. Seeing a need for expansion, Bishop Spangenburg began in 1752 to search for suitable land in North Carolina.

View down Main Street in Salem, settled by the Moravians in 1766. Today, visitors can see many restored homes and buildings at Old Salem in Winston Salem and at nearby Bethania and Bethabara.

He was not a young man; in fact, he was close to the half-century mark when he started his explorations, but he was wise in the ways of the frontier. Portly, with a receding hairline and a large nose, he had a kindly smile that illuminated his face, eyes that crinkled when he laughed, and sandy hair that he wore long in back. More important, he had great stamina and a resilient sense of humor. In addition, his serene confidence that God guided his steps through the wilderness made him an indomitable man setting out across the colony.

As the bishop rode into the Piedmont, he observed that some settlers were refugees from debt, some from courts or jails, and some from poverty. Several bands of thieves had moved into the back country and a number of farmers came because they heard livestock didn't have to be fed in winter. But Spangenburg heard that a better class of settlers was arriving.

His small surveying party trudged west, and the bliss of Indian summer changed to occasional sharp mornings and frigid nights. The Bishop increasingly worried about the living conditions that would face his beloved Moravians when they moved here. Although the Tuscarora Indians treated them kindly, he was objective enough to see future dangers, and he knew that beyond the coast settlers lived in constant fear of most Indian tribes.

"There are other things to make life hard for those living *alone* and *for themselves*," he noted. "For instance, a woman is ill, has high fever—where is the nurse, medicine, proper food? The wife of the nearest neighbor lives half a mile, perhaps several miles away; and she has her [own] children, her cattle, her own household to care for, and can give her only a couple of hours, or at most only one day or one night. . . . What will happen to those who have not the necessary talents [for the frontier]? What will they do in circumstances where each must help himself as best he can? How bear the hard work necessary to success, when each must say with Jacob, 'In the day the drought consumed me, and the frost by night?' To speak plainly, among fifty members brought up in our congregation or who have lived with us some years, there is probably not one who could maintain himself alone in the forest. . . . Perhaps it would be wise to settle six or ten families together, each in its own house, all working together under a capable overseer. . . ."

Near Blowing Rock winter set in. Spangenburg and his party had traveled farther than they had intended into the mountains. "A hunter, whom we had taken to show us the way, and who once knew the path to the [Yadkin] missed the trail, and led us into a place from where there was no way out except climbing an indescribably steep mountain. Part of the way we climbed on hands and knees, dragging after us the loads we had taken from the backs of the horses, for had we not unsaddled them, they would have fallen backwards down the mountains—indeed, this did happen once. Part of the way we led the horses, who were trembling like a leaf. When we reached the top, we saw mountains to right and to left, before and behind us, many hundreds of mountains, rising like great waves in a storm."

They went as far as Boone and, at last, in December were on their way back. Near the site of the present city of Winston-Salem, Brother Joseph found his Promised Land. He called it Wachovia after the German lands on which Moravians had first found refuge.

Following page: Children attend school in the Gemeinhaus at Bethabara.

On November 7, 1753, the first fifteen men arrived at the chosen site for the new town which they named Bethabara—House of Passage. Each man had special skills, for among them were a business manager, pastor, doctor, shoemaker, mill-wright, cooper, tailor, baker, and several carpenters and experienced farmers.

Bethabara grew quickly through their efforts. Within a few years individual houses had been built for a number of the men whose families joined them, as well as a storehouse and little shops in which the craftsmen could carry on their trades. Their gardens flourished, and they found that a wide variety of vegetables, herbs, and fruit trees grew well in the rich Piedmont soil. A thriving business soon developed at the congregation store, and their wagons traded in Brunswick and Charleston. In 1756 they built a high palisade around the perimeter of the main settlement as protection against Indians and wild animals.

The Cupola House in Edenton was owned by Francis Corbin in 1758. As Lord Granville's land agent, Corbin had angered a group of citizens who broke into his house on the night of January 23, 1759, and kidnaped him as his wife watched helplessly.

Anna Catherina Kalberlahn, who came to Bethabara as the bride of the settlement's doctor, recorded in her diary a conversation with a Cherokee. He told her that during the French and Indian War, which seethed around the little town and brought hundreds of refugees to the safety of the palisade, his tribe had planned to attack several times. However, each time as they crept from the woods, late at night or early in the morning, they would hear the blowing of a horn or the loud ringing of a bell which warned them, said the Indian, that they had been sighted by the alert Moravians. They gave up their plan. Actually, the citizens of Bethabara had been going about their usual routine, unaware of the Cherokees. The horn the Indians heard was that of the night watchman who blew his trumpet each hour as he made his rounds to signify that all was well. In the early morning, the church bell calling the community to morning prayers frightened the attackers away. "So does the Lord protect his Brethren!" wrote Anna Catherina.

Problems with the Indians were not the only concern of the frontier. Colonel John Frohock of Rowan County rode into Bethabara to collect the annual quitrent due Lord Granville's agent, Francis Corbin, an old acquaintance of Bishop Spangenburg's. The rent was promptly paid, but Colonel Frohock remarked that he was having great trouble collecting in other parts of the district.

He was not the only of Corbin's subordinates who was having difficulties. In 1755 a committee of the General Assembly, investigating complaints by landholders in the Granville District, reported that Corbin and his agents were "exacting exorbitant fees on all grants." As such reports continued, the legislature felt that ignorance of legal fees was at the heart of the problem, so they published the rates charged by Granville's men. Since little of this information filtered down to back country farmers, it was ineffective.

Finally, on the night of January 23, 1759, several dozen landholders of Halifax and Edgecombe counties saddled their horses to handle the matter directly. They set out for Edenton at dusk and rode up to the Cupola House. Mr. Corbin had purchased it recently and remodeled it in handsome fashion with the small fortune he was now amassing in fees, all of which he demanded in specie (hard money acceptable in London). In the flickering glow of their lightwood torches, the men broke into the house and kidnapped the petrified Corbin as his young wife watched helplessly. They rode away with him into the winter night and at Enfield threw him in jail along with Joshua Bodley, another of Granville's agents. After only a day or two, they were able to exact a promise from Corbin to adjust their tax levies and to appear at the next term of Granville Court to stand trial for extortion.

Corbin related that he was "frightened out of his wits," but back at Edenton, away from jail and his captors' gazes, he soon reverted to his old ways. Eventually he was removed from office, but Governor Dobbs and the Assembly apparently still sided with the agents. The inland farmer still found no relief from overcharges or seizures of his land for nonpayment of inflated rents.

The Pulse of Liberty Still Beats

The Homestead at Edenton, overlooking the Chowan River, was built by Robert Smith before the Revolution.

Wherever one traveled along the North Carolina seaboard that balmy spring of 1765, the topic of conversation was stamps. On the wharves of Edenton, New Bern, and Wilmington the town's merchants met each arriving sea captain to get the latest news. At Beaufort, the fishermen talked of the tax as they unloaded their day's catch, and even at Bath, where the port was becoming sadly empty as ships sailed farther up the Pamlico River in Beaufort County, the occasional seaman was eagerly questioned as his ship came through customs.

Over tea tables and in taverns, when voices raised to a high pitch of excitement, the subject of the speaker's wrath was the new tax proposed by Parliament. It was an *internal* tax! A tax about which the colonial assemblies had not been consulted! A tax that would touch every citizen! Every newspaper, as well as playing cards, tavern licenses, bills of lading, legal papers, mortgages, almanacs, and dice would have to bear the hated stamp! And it was payable only in specie, a rare item of exchange in an economy largely based on credit or barter.

Nevertheless, after a year of rumor and discussion and pleas by Thomas Barker, Benjamin Franklin, and other colonial agents to Lord Grenville and the Board of Trade, the despised bill was introduced in Parliament on February 13, 1765. The debate was routine. Every member knew that, with millions added to the national debt by the French and Indian War which had ended two years before, raising additional revenues was essential. Where could it be more logically raised than in the colonies? Surely the Americans could pay for their own defense!

One member, Colonel Isaac Barré, however, raised his irate voice in protest. In objecting to taxation without representation, he told his fellow members indignantly that the Americans were "sons of liberty," fighting for the cause of every Englishman!

The phrase rolled sonorously through the House of Commons and continued rolling across the stormy Atlantic in record time. In Boston, it caught the finely tuned ears of Sam Adams and James Otis and the Sons of Liberty was born.

It took little time for Barré's apt phrase and news of Boston's patriot organization to travel down the seacoast and along the Outer Banks to Cape Fear. Here it quickly struck a responsive chord with the second generation of The Family, sons of those pioneer Ashes, Moores, Moseleys, and Harnetts who fought the Indians, cleared the land, and began a booming trade in naval stores. They had inherited the spirit that had breathed life into the new town of Brunswick which in turn had wrested economic domination of the colony from the Albemarle. With this same enthusiasm, this second generation built vast plantations, a thriving mercantile business, and even took time out for culture—books, London papers, and the arts—which was an idle luxury in their fathers' day. They bought slaves and saw no inconsistency between this and their own independent natures. No less than the founders, they had a vital interest in politics, taking their seats in the General Assembly or Governor's Council and serving in the militia.

By spring, indignant at Parliament's attempt to wrest the right of taxation from colonial legislatures, they had formed a Cape Fear chapter of the Sons of Liberty. The prime mover was Cornelius Harnett, Jr., who had moved upriver to Wilmington where he had developed a large mercantile business. Other sons of The Family took leading roles—John and Samuel Ashe and Robert Howe—as did relatives of the Moores. Two like-minded Cape Fear men, Abner Nash and Hugh Waddell, also participated.

They were a formidable group and behind them rallied the owners of small shops, craftsmen, sailors, and farmers—the unsophisticated men who never wore a powdered wig. Their pocketbooks were touched and tempers were short as the long arm of British government began to meddle with their freedom. North Carolinians felt few pangs over England's war debts. They had sent their share of militia under Hugh Waddell to fight the French and Indian War and had voted more money for defense than circulated in the colony. The members of the Sons of Liberty in Carolina, unlike their New England brothers, never had a secret organization. Its leaders put their names and their considerable financial investments on the line when they opposed British policy as they had done since the previous year when the Currency and Sugar acts were passed.

During this period of unrest, thirty-six-year-old William Tryon, his retinue, his wife, and his daughter arrived in Brunswick where the ailing Governor Arthur Dobbs resided. Dobbs was expected to retire upon Tryon's arrival from London, but the grand old man had no such intention. He remained governor until his death in April. Tryon, his duties as deputy governor being light, had time to become familiar with the currents and cross-currents of feeling among the people before he took over as governor.

There was little doubt about majority opinion on taxation. Five months before Parliament met to consider the Stamp Act, the North Carolina Assembly had gone on record as opposing internal taxation of the colonies as being "against what we esteem our inherent right and exclusive privilege of imposing our own taxes."

Tryon was wise enough to overlook the optimistic views of his Royalist friends. Instead he asked Assembly Speaker John Ashe how he felt the colony would react to the Stamp Act. Ashe replied with complete candor, "We will resist it to the death."

There was no personal animosity in this. The Cape Fear men liked the new governor and he liked them. He was well educated, well read, with the advantage of nineteen years as an

Greenfield, near Edenton, was called Fordice's when it was built in the mid-1700s in the popular West Indies style of the period. *Facing page:* The Leigh House, Edenton, was built about 1759 by Gilbert Leigh. Two signers of the Edenton Tea Party Resolutions lived there—Lydia Bennett and, later, Sara Valentine.

army officer to prepare him for leadership; even before he arrived, he had started work on a progressive program of road building and of improved mail service for the colony. He and his attractive wife, Margaret, had considerable charm and made friends easily. It was simply a matter of principle and tradition for the Cape Fear men to oppose a policy that encroached on their liberties, and it was William Tryon's principle to stand behind his government even when he privately felt its judgment was mistaken.

In late April, word reached North Carolina that the act had passed. It was to go into effect November 1 under the direction of stamp masters appointed by the Crown. By early June the indignant Massachusetts legislature had sent a message to each colony urging them to send delegates to a Stamp Act Congress to be held in New York that October to discuss joint action that might be taken. Forewarned and seeing no reason to get embroiled with a legislature he knew only slightly and certainly would have to oppose, Tryon decided to handle the matter simply. He refused to call a meeting of the Assembly in time for them to elect delegates to the October meeting.

The matter was not so easily ended. He could prevent the official meeting, but he could not prevent the spontaneous public demonstrations that erupted throughout the summer and on into fall. At New Bern and Edenton and as far west as Cross Creek, the people gathered in protest.

By the time the dogwood trees turned red and the sweet gums golden, feeling in the Cape Fear area ran high, for shipping, its life blood, would soon be taxed. The proximity of the Tryons at Russellborough and in Brunswick of Dr. William Houston, who was to be appointed stamp-master, acted as a constant reminder.

Cornelius Harnett, Jr., called several urgent meetings of the Sons of Liberty to discuss various plans for opposing the act.

Although some of the more conservative merchants considered the members to be "radicals," there was nothing of the blazing-eyed fanatic about Harnett. More sophisticated than his father, who had engaged in name-calling and fisticuffs with two proprietary governors in his youth, he had a reputation for making thoughtful, forceful decisions. He had a robust sense of humor developed at his father's Brunswick tavern where a serious demeanor was never a trait of The Family or the frontier travelers who drank their Jamaica rum there.

Harnett was slight, wiry, energetic, of medium height, and forty-two years old when the Stamp Act was passed. His only son, Cornelius III, had died as a small child about twenty years before, a sorrow that stabbed him occasionally when he and his wife, Mary Holt, were alone at Hilton. Its walls could easily have held many sons and daughters comfortably.

He and Mary were members of St. James Church in Wilmington, and he was an active Mason. Governor Johnston had appointed him Justice of the Peace in 1750, and the same year he was named as a town commissioner. In 1754, the voters of New Hanover County elected him to the General Assembly, and he had been reelected each year.

On October 19, a Saturday market day in Wilmington, the Sons of Liberty put their first plan into action. By seven o'clock in the evening about five hundred people had gathered in front of the courthouse. An effigy of Lord Bute was brought out (a case of mistaken identity—it should have been Lord Grenville). The crowd cheered; small boys jumped up and down and whistled loudly. A rope was tossed over the limb of the nearest tree and Bute, lumpily stuffed with straw, was ingloriously hanged by the neck.

Excitement grew feverish as several of the men built a large bonfire nearby and doused the straw man with tar. A spark was struck to the tinder, crimson fire leaped high into the autumn night, and the effigy of the hapless Bute was consigned to the flames.

In case any pro-British citizen had missed the ceremony by accident or intent, the Sons of Liberty moved quickly from house to house, firmly knocked on each door, and politely requested to see the men of the house—in tones that made the request a demand. Then appeared the reluctant or red faces of annoyed merchants, their teen-age sons, and a few gray-haired old men, cloaked in belligerent dignity. With little ceremony, these gentlemen were escorted to the bonfire and handed a brimming drink mixed more to a seaman's taste than a lace-cuffed aristocrat's.

Cornelius Harnett raised his glass high. "A toast!" he called out in a voice that could stir a loafing dockworker from high on a quarterdeck. "Drink up, gentlemen. To Liberty, Property, and no Stamp Duty!"

In the smoky half-light, glasses were raised with varying degrees of enthusiasm as the coattails of the tar-splashed effigy curled into ashes. The last of the potent rum from each glass burned its way down.

"And another!" cried one of Liberty's sons, who may well have been John Ashe. "I give you the confusion of Lord Bute and all his like-minded friends!"

Another hearty draft drained glasses, mugs, and tankards alike. Three loud "Hurrahs"

Following page:
From homes like these came men who formed the Regulators
in an effort to force the eastern-dominated Assembly
to consider the problems of the back country.

rang out after each toast in a medley of five hundred voices. And the bottles were passed around again to those strong enough to continue.

The ceremony, according to Andrew Steuart's *North Carolina Gazette,* continued "until 12 of the Clock, and then dispersed without doing any Mischief."

Just about the time the gossip concerning this affair died down, All Hallows' Eve approached. Harnett and the Sons of Liberty, noting that the Stamp Act would go into effect the following day, decided the night was good for someone besides spirits to be abroad. This time they made an effigy of Liberty herself which, the *Gazette* reported, "they put into a coffin, and marched in solemn procession . . . to the church-yard, a drum in mourning beating before them, and the town bell, muffled, ringing a doleful knell at the same time."

Their mourning was premature, the crowd soon discovered with delight, for one of the procession's leaders thought to check the pulse of the supposed corpse. He announced to the cheering townspeople that Liberty still had a faint heartbeat!

Quickly they carried her along Market Street in an armchair back to a lighted bonfire and "concluded the evening with great rejoicings on finding that Liberty still had an existence in the colonies."

Like all mornings after, dawn broke with less than festivity in the air. Ships rocked silently at their piers, the wind rattling in their rigging. Clearance papers for the ships could not be stamped because not one stamp had yet arrived in the colony. Several newspapers suspended publication briefly and then within a few weeks appeared again with a skull and crossbones printed at the top where a stamp should have been. Courts were closed. Couples could not be married or land or houses sold. Taverns could not legally serve liquor, although it is not recorded that any refused to do so, especially with every seafaring man in town on an enforced holiday!

At Brunswick, Dr. Houston still had not received official word of his appointment as stamp-master although he and the entire province knew in a matter of time word would come. On November 16, he rode into Wilmington for a visit. Word of his arrival spread through town like wildfire, and almost out of nowhere, several hundred people appeared at the house where he had taken a room. Flags were unfurled, and a drummer beat a martial rat-a-tat-tat. When Dr. Houston appeared, the crowd demanded to know whether or not he intended to carry out the duties of his office.

"I should be very sorry to execute any office disagreeable to the people of the province," the *Gazette* reported the good doctor as replying tactfully. To make his words binding, however, several strong Sons of Liberty carried Dr. Houston to the courthouse and forced him to sign a resignation. Then, according to the *Gazette's* observant reporter, the people escorted the former stamp master around the square and gave him three cheers at every corner.

That evening another large bonfire blazed in celebration at the courthouse. A table "well furnished with several sorts of liquors" was set up in the firelight, and the assembled company drank "all the favorite American toasts" in fine fettle.

Governor Tryon got word of this latest episode while sick in bed at Russellborough. Although he undoubtedly felt much worse after hearing the news, he roused himself enough to send invitations to the leading citizens of New Hanover, Brunswick, Duplin, and Bladen counties to join him for dinner on November 18. He reasoned that if he could get the cooperation of these influential gentlemen before the stamps arrived, he might have some hopes of keeping the situation on an even keel.

About fifty distinguished merchants and office holders attended and ate a sumptuous meal from the governor's imported china. They drank his best wine and listened politely to his request to permit the stamps to be circulated as the law required. Tryon did not touch on the principle of taxation that was involved because this was beyond his domain, but it was his responsibility to enforce the law. He offered to purchase personally the wine licenses for a number of taverns in various towns and to pay from his own pocket the tax on any documents on which he, as the royal governor, would receive a fee.

Apparently his guests did not wish to appear ungrateful while under his roof for they made no reply, but the next day they sent him a letter in which they stated that they felt it would be "securer conduct" to do their best to prevent the operation of any aspect of the Stamp Act. It was a succinct way of stating a fact—their businesses and elective offices were indeed more secure from the anger of the Sons of Liberty as long as they did not actively oppose that group's political views.

On November 28, the sloop of war *Diligence* arrived at the port of Brunswick by way of Virginia with the first cargo of stamped paper from England. At the helm was her master, Constantine John Phipps, a genial naval officer and Arctic explorer who had received a friendly welcome there many times. When he weighed anchor, a nearby fisherman called the news to him that Colonels Waddell and Ashe with a large company of militia were waiting on shore to resist any landing of the stamps. Captain Phipps could hardly believe his ears, but when the fisherman added that the two officers, whom Phipps knew by reputation if not personally, had said they would fire on anyone attempting to land the stamps, he decided not to unload them.

The members of the Sons of Liberty were not entirely appeased. Just to be sure Captain Phipps didn't change his mind, they seized one of the *Diligence's* boats, mounted it on a cart, and merrily rolled it to Wilmington, leaving a small party on guard at the Brunswick docks. That night they marched into town triumphantly to a grand illumination, efficiently organized by the Sons of Liberty to celebrate its victory. Lanterns or candles shone from every window as though it were the king's birthday.

On January 2 Captain Jacob Lobb of the British *Viper* seized two merchant ships, the *Dobbs* and the *Patience*, which sailed into Brunswick from Philadelphia where stamps were no more recognized than in Carolina. He delivered their unstamped ships' papers to Port Collector William Dry and ordered him to institute proceedings against the two masters in Vice Admiralty Court. No man to stick his neck out, Collector Dry in turn asked the attorney

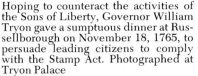

Hoping to counteract the activities of the Sons of Liberty, Governor William Tryon gave a sumptuous dinner at Russellborough on November 18, 1765, to persuade leading citizens to comply with the Stamp Act. Photographed at Tryon Palace

general to investigate and report what should be done. Before the attorney general could act, another merchantman, the *Ruby*, arrived and was also boarded and its papers seized. In a tit-for-tat move, the Sons of Liberty refused to sell supplies to the hungry men of the *Viper* and threw into jail the crew of a bumboat caught trying to do so.

In February the attorney general's decision that Captain Lobb's seizure was indeed legal and the ships' masters should be sent to Nova Scotia for trial brought matters to a climax.

The Sons of Liberty refused to sit idly by while such "justice" took its course. The members called a mass meeting in Wilmington on February 18 of freeholders from Brunswick, New Hanover, Duplin, and Bladen counties. Here with Harnett, Waddell, and Ashe in the fore, they signed an agreement saying that "we will at any risk . . . unite . . . in preventing entirely the operation of the Stamp Act."

The next day several hundred of them bearing arms (mostly hunting rifles) marched to Brunswick where they broke open the desk of Collector Dry and stole the seized papers. Then they surrounded nearby Russellborough. A little after 6:00 p.m., Cornelius Harnett and George Moore (son of Roger) delivered a letter to the governor personally, assuring him they meant him no harm or insult. Harnett explained, "We are marching in hopes of obtaining a peaceful means of redress of our grievances from the commanding officers of His Majesty's ships." They courteously offered to provide a guard to protect the governor and his property.

Examples of the fine craftsmanship of
Salem and Bethabara metal workers
still adorn their homes, churches, and
shops.

William Tryon replied indignantly, "I hope your protection will *not* be given, whether it is needed or desired!" He then showed Harnett and Moore to the door. Harnett walked thoughtfully across the piazza which surrounded the house and down the steps to the walk. For a moment he stood looking at the river through the winter-bare branches of the tall trees. He had played along these banks as a little boy; for a moment he longed for those more peaceful days—if such they were. He wished Tryon had accepted his offer of a guard. These Sons of Liberty that he headed were not always as restrained as he might have wished. They weren't vicious, but they were impulsive, and the anger they felt at the seizure of merchant ships which in many cases supplied their livelihoods (as well as his own) was not always easy to control. Well, the next few days would tell the tale.

By the morning of the 20th, hundreds of additional armed men from nearby counties had joined them, making a total of close to a thousand. His own attitude, Harnett knew, would set the pace. Could he keep his own reserve and judgment?

Very early that day a delegation boarded the *Viper* and ordered Captain Lobb to release the merchant ships. The governor, whose patience had reached the breaking point, had told Lobb to resist, but the captain had had enough from this aroused citizenry. He gave in.

That night, Customs Comptroller Pennington, from whom the protesters wanted a guarantee against future seizures, fled swiftly along the shadowy road to Russellborough to ask Tryon for a bed for the night, safe from his pursuers. (The story was more frequently told among the militia that he hid *under* the governor's bed!) Shortly after dawn, the aroused citizens gathered outside, and a company of sixty, with Harnett marching at their head, came up to the front door.

Governor Tryon came out to meet them, and Harnett asked to see Pennington. Tryon refused to produce him. Then Harnett "standing face to face and eye to eye with the governor" informed him quickly that unless the comptroller appeared, the people would take him by force.

The alarmed Pennington had been listening inside. Now he came to the door. "I have decided to go with these gentlemen, sir," he told Tryon with a glance at the mob in the road.

"In that case," said the governor scornfully, "give me your resignation first!"

"That's not necessary," Harnett put in, anxious to end the matter as quickly as possible. The governor gave him a withering glance and continued to wait. "Sir, you now have my resignation," Pennington said meekly. Then he turned and followed Harnett down the steps and into Brunswick. There he and the public officials involved, surrounded by a circle of cheering patriots, signed an oath that they would never issue any stamped paper in North Carolina. Without a single shot being fired, the fight had been won. Cornelius Harnett became known as "the Pride of the Cape Fear."

In England, the colonists' refusal to use the stamps showed up in a telling form. The resultant breakdown in colonial trade caused a severe depression. British merchants and manufacturers cried to Parliament for relief. By March the disputed act was repealed.

In North Carolina and throughout the colonies, the happy news was greeted with the ringing of church bells and a lifting of spirits. Ships sailed again, courts opened, and the sale of real estate was resumed. The moral victory was even sweeter than the specific one. The colonists had protested, and Parliament had been forced to back down. But many Americans had forgotten to read the fine print. Along with the repeal of the Stamp Act, Parliament had passed a Declaratory Resolution asserting that it still had the right to tax its American colonies.

Among the cheers that went up at the repeal of the Stamp Act was a significant one from the farmers of Sandy Creek in Orange County. They sent a resolve to the General Assembly combining their congratulations with what could only be construed as a warning:

"While the Sons of Liberty withstood the Lords in Parliament in behalf of true liberty, let not officers under them carry on unjust oppression in our own province.... Take this as a maxim, that while men are men, though you should see all the Sons of Liberty set in office and vested with power, they would soon corrupt again and oppress, if they were not called upon to give an account of their stewardship."

The Orange County landholders made a diplomatic error though. They sent their message via a county assemblyman, Edmund Fanning of Hillsborough. The Sandy Creek men, dissatisfied with certain county officials, asked them to attend the next meeting to discuss their qualifications for office and to hear some problems Sandy Creek would like to have presented to the General Assembly.

Fanning declared such a meeting to be "insurrectionary" and ordered his officers not to attend or to allow these people to question them before "the bar of their shallow understanding." Fanning was no lover of the common man. He was a native of New York, in his late twenties, a classics graduate of Yale, and a close friend of Governor Tryon. He might have felt at home on the eastern seaboard, but in the back country surrounding the small town of Hillsborough, with its unpaved streets lined principally with log cabins, he was a fish out of water.

He was an easy target for the jibes of his constituents. What did he know of the backache a man got from hoeing his cornfield, chopping in and out among the tree stumps all day? Or the crying of hungry children when bears broke into the garden or drought set back the crops? Or the fear of a lone woman when the sheriff hammered at her door unexpectedly, demanding his taxes in hard money and her with not a shilling in the house? What did he know of the satisfaction a man had in riding up to his house with a deer slung over the back of his horse to cut up into fine venison steaks or to salt down for the winter? Whose "bar of understanding" was shallow? The Orange County men thought it was Edmund Fanning's.

The moderate faction at Sandy Creek was discouraged into temporary silence by officials who took the position that they weren't responsible to the people. In a peculiar but legal way they were right. Under colonial law, the governor and his council appointed justices of the

Skillful Salem women spun and dyed yarn from wool sheared from their sheep. With it they stitched exquisite crewel work such as the delicate patterns shown on the frame and bedspread in the tavern keeper's bedroom.

peace in each county who levied county and parish taxes and controlled almost every element of local government, including the appointment of sheriffs. These officials were not paid by salary, but by fees which they frequently inflated above the legal amount.

The legislature was not eager to pass reforms, for two-thirds of the assemblymen were also justices of the peace, and other multiple office-holding was commonplace. Edmund Fanning, in addition to being a lawyer and member of the Assembly, was a registrar, superior court judge, and colonel of the militia. John Frohock was assemblyman, clerk, justice of the peace, member of the county court, and also a colonel in the militia.

In the General Assembly western freeholders were represented by only one man for each 7,300 people, while easterners had one delegate for each 1,700. To add to the political clout of the coast at this time, all members of the Governor's Council, all judges, the treasurer, and the Speaker of the House were from the east. In addition, back country men had no substitute for cash but the barter system, and taxes and quitrents were payable only in specie. Tryon had already written to Lord Hillsborough explaining the lack of currency in the colony and asking permission to issue paper money. His request was denied.

Tryon was also fully aware that back country complaints against dishonest sheriffs who not only overcharged but neglected to pay the required amount into the colonial treasury were legitimate. He estimated that sheriffs embezzled one-half the tax money they collected! Since the treasurer was elected by popular vote, and the sheriff presided at elections, the latter was seldom reminded of his arrears.

In 1767, frustrated by this stalemate, William Tryon was glad of an excuse to travel west where his visit might show an interest in the Piedmont. He would survey the southern boundary line and establish a treaty line with the Cherokees beyond which white home-steaders would not be allowed to settle. He set off for the west with his wife, Margaret, and a large retinue on May 18.

At the foothills of the Blue Ridge, Tryon met with the Cherokees and set the first mountain range as the boundary for white settlement. The Cherokees gave him the Indian name of "Great Wolf," a high honor since it had been the name of several of their most distinguished chiefs.

Turning eastward again, the Tryon party stopped at Bethabara for a weekend visit. Rain

The earliest houses in Salem were of half-timber construction.

Today a tinsmith works at making candle sconces in much the same way Philip Reich made them almost a century and a half ago.

was misting as they approached town, but the pastor and several musicians rode out to escort them. The stirring sound of trumpets and French horns announced their arrival. Rooms had been prepared at the home of the tailor, and a delicious meal of buttered vegetables fresh from the garden, roasted meats fragrant with herbs, and crusty bread hot from the oven was served at the Brothers House.

The next day they rode through the woods to see the progress being made in building Salem, the new town whose name meant "peace." Several wives rode with them at Mrs. Tryon's suggestion. Much impressed, they returned and visited the mill and several craft shops. The governor was so delighted by the quality of their products that he ordered a large number of candles, butter, tallow, flour, and zwieback to be delivered to him by the Moravians' next wagon to Brunswick.

What a joy to find this flourishing community of loyal subjects in this region where reports indicated all was chaos. He urged Brother Graff to apply for representation in the General Assembly, but the Moravian told him they feared other nearby settlers would be jealous if they did so. Lookng around the thriving town with its sturdy houses, craft shops and stores, neat gardens, and hardworking people, the governor could not suppress a smile.

"They will be jealous of you in any case," he counseled Brother Graff. "So it would be better if they were jealous *and* you had representation!"

On Sunday morning, the Tryons joined Bethabara citizens for services at the Gemeinhaus. The governor listened with interest as the doctrine of the Moravian church was explained: "In essentials—unity; in nonessentials—liberty; and in all things—charity." The Anglican governor nodded in understanding. The choir joyfully sang to the accompaniment of the little pipe organ so carefully brought by boat from Philadelphia to Wilmington and then overland by wagon to Bethabara.

After dinner Mrs. Tryon could not resist going back to play the organ herself. A number of the Single Sisters gathered around and sang as she played. Even the governor, attracted from his room by the singing and laughter, came in to hum an accompaniment.

The next morning they were to leave for the coast again, and that night a group of musicians played softly under the Tryons' window at bedtime. Then through the still night they heard the trumpet of the watchman on his rounds signaling that all was well.

The interlude was pleasant to remember, especially since Tryon arrived back at Brunswick to angry outcries from the back country over the expense of his expedition. Additional furor broke when that fall the General Assembly appropriated £10,000 in addition to the £5,000 already earmarked for construction in New Bern of a permanent seat of government, popularly called "Tryon Palace." So determined was Tryon to accomplish this, after decades of false starts by previous governors, that he had brought with him to America an outstanding architect, John Hawkes, who had been a surveyor of St. Paul's Cathedral in London. Hawkes designed a central brick building with a ground floor and two upper stories connected with two wings by curving colonnades. When completed it would be called "the most beautiful

The Salem gunsmith rifles a barrel in his shop at the Single Brothers House.
Because the Moravians' religion forbade bearing arms in war, their rifles were used only for hunting.

public building in the colonies." It would house not only the residence of the royal governor but the public records, an assembly hall, council chamber, and public offices.

Protests from the back country were as thick as acorns on an oak tree. The protesters called it unnecessary, extravagant, and said not one man out of twenty in the four most populous counties (all in the west) would ever see it, let alone get any use from it.

Printer James Davis defended it in the *North Carolina Gazette:* "Can you see the *Public Records* carted from place to place, and your properties and estates trusted to the mercy of a shower of rain, and at the discretion of a cart driver? Forbid it Heaven!"

In 1768 western farmers formally organized "The Regulators," and declared they would pay no more taxes or fees until they saw the legal amounts allowable and how they were spent. County officials denounced the demands and refused to comply. In April a sheriff in Orange County seized a farmer's mare for unpaid taxes and rode off with it to Hillsborough. A few hours later, a group of Regulators followed, took back the horse, and as they rode out of town, fired into the roof of Fanning's house "to signify they blamed him for all this abuse."

Fanning, a man of words, instantly drew his pen and wrote to Governor Tryon that "the late orderly and well-regulated County of Orange, is now (O my favourite county and people, how art thou fallen!) the very nest and bosom of rioting and rebellion." Unable to restrain his

sense of drama, he wrote that he expected at any moment to be attacked by the entire rebel force and had determined "to bravely repulse them or nobly die."

The governor took his friend at face value and issued two proclamations—one ordering the Regulators to disperse, and the other calling the militia to be in readiness to march to Fanning's aid.

On May 21, 1768, the Regulators, led by Herman Husband, a Pennsylvania-born Quaker and disciple of Benjamin Franklin, James Hunter, and poet Rednap Howell drew up a new summary of their grievances which they took to Governor Tryon. Known as Regulator Advertisement #11, it expressed their loyalty to the Crown and blamed their troubles on the corrupt practices of "nefarious men." It also apologized for the men who fired into Fanning's roof.

Tryon told them the issues did not justify what amounted to mob rule. He ordered them to give up their organized activities and pay the taxes they had withheld. However, he also conferred with his council and issued a warning to county officials and lawyers against taking excessive fees, published a list of legal charges, and ordered his attorney general to prosecute any individual accused of extortion. Tryon also told Husband that he would be in Hillsborough for the summer term of court where he hoped to find everything peaceful.

In August the governor took his family with him to Hillsborough, where he found his arrival met with rumors on both sides. The Regulators heard he was bringing the militia against them from the east and inciting the Cherokees to attack from the west. He, in turn, heard that the Regulators *en masse* were about to march to Hillsborough and rescue William Butler and Husband. Fanning had arrested the two "for inciting the populace to rebellion" and they were due to be tried at court. Consequently, Tryon did muster the militia and the Regulators did gather to attend the court.

The presiding judge was Maurice Moore, who managed to keep a cool head in spite of the milling 1,461 militiamen and Regulators who (according to Husband) numbered 3,700.

The Salem potter makes bowls and dishes, stove tiles and pipes from clay found nearby. At the tavern, a coin unlocks the "Honesty Box" to provide tobacco for the gentleman's clay pipe.

Husband was tried and acquitted. Butler and two other Regulators were fined and sentenced to jail, but the governor commuted their sentences and suspended payment of the fines for three months. Fanning, tried on a charge of extortion as a result of the governor's order, was found guilty though he pleaded ignorance of the fact that the legal fee for which he charged six shillings was only two shillings and eight pence. He was fined "one penny and costs." Humiliated, he resigned his office, although this still left him with three or four others.

The "Battle of the Eno" evaporated like dew, and the Regulators and militia marched quietly home. Yet, the Regulators complained that this show of force had cost the province an unnecessary £4,500.

Hope rose in the back country in 1769 when almost solid Regulator delegations were elected from Orange, Granville, Halifax, and Anson counties. When the General Assembly opened in October, Herman Husband, one of the new delegates, presented his petitions for reform. He asked for elections by ballot, replacement of the poll tax with a property tax, salaries to be paid chief justices instead of fees, a limit placed on clerks' fees, small debt claims to be heard in court without a lawyer, and additional policy changes. But in four days—before these petitions were put into form for a vote—Governor Tryon dissolved the Assembly. The action looked like a slap at the western delegates, but it was not. Lord Hillsborough had ordered it for an entirely different reason. A vote was expected on the issue of the Townshend duties, an import tax on wine, glass, lead, paint, and tea. Tryon opposed the Townshend Act also and was promptly reprimanded by Parliament for doing so. Hillsborough, whose diplomatic efforts managed to save Tryon's reputation at home, advised him to dissolve the next Assembly before it could take action on a proposed nonimportation agreement among the colonies. Tryon did so, and as a result, the more pressing problem of the Regulators remained unsolved. However, John Harvey called for a meeting "independent of the Governor," and sixty-four of the sixty-seven assemblymen met at the New Bern

The Old Town Clock in the Hillsborough Courthouse marked time on court days as the Regulators swarmed into town to protest. The clock is said to have been a gift of the Earl of Hillsborough for whom Tryon named the town.

courthouse the next day and drew up a "nonimportation association" which they circulated throughout the colony. Prime Minister Lord North exclaimed, "The drunken ragamuffins of a vociferous mob are exalted into equal importance with men of judgment, morals, and property. I can never acquiesce in the absurd opinion that all men are equal!" The next year, Parliament repealed all but the tea tax.

In September 1770 the fire smouldering in the back country erupted into flames at the Hillsborough Court where the docket was filled with cases for and against the rebellious landholders. When Judge Richard Henderson called court to order, part of the 150 Regulators "shouting, hallooing and making a considerable tumult in the streets" swarmed into the courtroom until all the seats were filled. Those outside attacked a late arrival, Attorney John Williams, and then surged inside to assault William Hooper of Wilmington, now deputy attorney general. They "dragged and paraded [Hooper] through the streets." Lawyer Fanning, who had hidden behind the judge's bench when the rioting started, was pulled outside by his heels and beaten until, as the judge told it, "by a manly exertion [he] miraculously broke hold and jumped into a door that saved him from immediate dissolution."

Judge Henderson in a futile gesture adjourned court and ran in terror out of town as the Regulators in high glee took over, held a mock court, and tried their own cases in raucous fashion. Then, swept along by mob hysteria, they broke into Fanning's house, destroyed his papers and furniture, and set the house on fire.

As the Regulators dispersed, the hills and valleys rang with one of Rednap Howell's most popular new ballads:

> *Said Frohock to Fanning, to tell the plain truth,*
> *When I came to this country, I was but a youth;*
> *My father sent for me; I warn't worth a cross,*
> *And then my first study was to cheat for a horse.*
> *I quickly got credit and strait ran away*
> *And haven't paid for him to this very day....*

Even barefoot children, as they spooned up their turnip salad cooked with pork and munched their corn pone that night, grinned as they joined in the singing, banging in rhythm with their pewter spoons on the table.

> *When Fanning first to Orange came*
> *He look'd both pale and wan;*
> *An old patch'd coat upon his back,*
> *An old mare he rode on.*
> *Both man and mare warn't worth five pounds*
> *As I've been often told;*
> *But by his civil robberies*
> *He's laced his coat with gold.*

Completed in 1770, Tryon Palace was virtually destroyed by fire in 1798. Today, it has been completely restored and attracts numerous visitors each year to examine its authentic furnishings and *(following page)* to enjoy its splendid garden.

Their "victory" was sweet but short. The Regulators had forced Tryon's hand. He was a career army man and Viceroy of the Crown in North Carolina. He could not permit anarchy.

The Assembly met on December 5 and expelled Herman Husband, jailing him in New Bern for libel. Though they rushed through much of the legislation he had introduced at the previous session, they also passed an emergency bill proposed by Samuel Johnston. (In the back country it was called "The Bloody Act.") It made rioting in any circuit court a crime which could be prosecuted in any county, regardless of where it occurred; authorized the governor to use military force to put down the Regulators; and outlawed any person resisting or avoiding arrest. (Several years later the Privy Council in London ruled that the law was completely unconstitutional.)

Panic gripped the east coast as word spread that the Regulators were marching on New Bern to free Herman Husband. The grand jury dismissed the charge against him, and he was released, but the rumors persisted. When news of the Johnston Act reached the back country, the Regulators responded by forbidding any future sessions of court and declared that Fanning and all other lawyers and judges should be killed on sight.

Governor Tryon had already received word of his new appointment as governor of New York, and Josiah Martin had arrived in this country to take his place. However, in North Carolina William Tryon had unfinished business. He called a special term of court to be held in Hillsborough and ordered out the militia to protect the session. He marched from the coast with 1,068 men — among them Cornelius Harnett, Hugh Waddell, Maurice Moore, William Hooper, Richard Caswell, John Ashe, and other Sons of Liberty. In the back country they were joined by the militia from Orange, Rowan, and several other western counties. They camped at Great Alamance Creek, near present-day Burlington.

On May 16, 1771, a force of about 2,000 Regulators confronted them and asked to talk to the governor. Tryon refused to negotiate until they gave up their arms and dispersed. He gave them an hour to do so. Herman Husband had already ridden away bound for Pennsylvania. James Hunter, a captain in the militia, was asked to take command of the ill-equipped and thoroughly untrained farmers, but he blandly refused, saying, "We are all free men, and everyone must command himself!"

The hour passed. The governor sent an officer to get their reply. It was succinct: "Fire and be damned!" At last Tryon gave the order to fire. There was silence. The militia, facing their own countrymen reluctantly, still hoped the Regulators would back down. At last Tryon rose in his stirrups, and riding the length of the field in front of them, cried out, "Fire! Fire on them, or fire at me!" The battle began.

The *Massachusetts Spy* of June 20, 1771, which received the report by express rider from North Carolina, takes up the story. "The Regulators to the number of at least 2,500 immediately formed with 20 or 30 paces distance and behaved in a most daring and desperate manner." For a few minutes it was touch and go, as the Regulators drove off the artillery gunners and captured one of their guns. Then, "the Regulators being hard pressed by our men . . . gave way on all sides, and were pursued to the distance of a mile through the woods

Below—top row, left: Desserts being made in the kitchen at Tryon Palace; *right:* Governor's bedchamber. *Bottom row, left:* Coachman's room; *right:* Secretary's office.

and bushes, our troops making great slaughter among them as they did not make a regular retreat, but ran in great confusion. . . ."

After two terrifying hours nine Regulators were dead and a larger number wounded. The militia had lost an equal number with sixty-one wounded. The *Spy* continues: "Twenty or thirty [Regulators] were made prisoners, and chief of their ammunition and baggage, consisting of hunting shirts, wallets of dumplings, jackets, breaches, powder-horns, and shot bags, were taken along with a number of horses. . . ."

Of those prisoners taken, twelve Regulators were tried for treason in Hillsborough, six of whom were pardoned by Tryon. The other six were hanged in Hillsborough on June 19 and buried in an unmarked grave by the Eno River. The governor offered clemency to all Regulators who laid down their arms and took an oath of allegiance to the Crown. Hundreds did so. Hundreds of others simply packed their belongings and moved farther west.

Triumphant William Tryon, his family, and a new private secretary—Edmund Fanning sailed out from Cape Fear on June 30; his successor, Josiah Martin, his wife Elizabeth, and eight young children arrived a few days later. In August Martin was officially sworn in as Royal Governor at the handsome new palace in New Bern. In the summer heat, a tragic fever epidemic swept the town, taking the life of one of the Martin children. The governor postponed his first meeting with the General Assembly until November when the epidemic had run its course. From the beginning, Martin and the legislature saw nothing eye to eye. After a series of moves and countermoves, they adjourned and Martin refused to call them into session again until January 1773. Here they tangled again over the colony's right to impound local property of British merchants who defaulted on their debts to North Carolinians, a rider attached to a routine renewal of a superior court bill. Since Martin would not pass it (the Crown having forbidden such action), nor the Assembly modify it, no higher courts could open—a stalemate that remained throughout the term of his office.

One observer of this strange situation was Josiah Quincy, Jr., of Boston, a member of the Sons of Liberty who traveled to the Cape Fear that spring for his health. "The present state of North Carolina is really curious," he wrote in his journal. "There are but five provincial laws in force throughout the colony, and no courts at all in being. No one can recover a debt, except before a single magistrate, where the sums are within his jurisdiction; and offenders escape with impunity. The people are in great consternation. . . ."

At Wilmington Quincy renewed his acquaintance with former Bostonian William Hooper and told him of Sam Adams' suggestion to form a Committee of Correspondence to exchange news and opinions in all the colonies. Quincy recorded: "Dined with about twenty at Mr. William Hooper's. . . . Spent the night at Mr. Harnett's—the Samuel Adams of North Carolina (except in point of fortune). . . . The plan of continental correspondence highly relished, ..."

In December the Assembly officially selected its Committee of Correspondence: Robert Howe, John Harvey, Samuel Johnston, Richard Caswell, John Ashe, Edward Vail, and Joseph Hewes. The Committees of Correspondence produced consternation in royal circles. In the tradition of free Englishmen, it was hard to accuse them. Forbid a group of gentlemen to write letters? They were an extralegal body—how could a governor dissolve them? They exchanged the news—did London papers do less? Yet in a real sense, they were uniting the thirteen colonies in resistance.

The British flag flies in front of the Thomas Barker House in Edenton as it did in 1774, when his wife Penelope helped organize the Edenton Tea Party. *Right:* Reenactment photographed in the Cupola House where the Penelope Barker portrait overlooks the ceremony.

That spring Parliament had passed the Tea Act, giving its ailing industry, the East India Company, a monopoly on the American market at the expense of colonial merchants. Boston's Sons of Liberty replied by boarding a British tea ship on December 16 and dumping her cargo—worth £15,000—into the harbor. In swift retribution, Parliament closed Boston harbor, annulled the colony's charter, and quartered its redcoats in private homes.

From all over North Carolina food for the beleaguered city poured into Wilmington where the sloop *Penelope* set sail, loaded with 2,095 bushels of corn, 22 barrels of flour, and 17 barrels of pork for beleaguered Bostonians.

Josiah Martin, hearing that a Continental Congress had been called for September in Philadelphia, indignantly refused to convene the Assembly to elect delegates. John Harvey, now an old hand at circumventing such action, simply announced, "In that case, the people will hold a convention independent of the governor." In Wilmington, Cornelius Harnett, Will Hooper, and several others called a mass meeting in support of Harvey's plan and issued an invitation for delegates to convene August 23 at New Bern under the governor's nose.

The First Provincial Congress—the first elected assembly held in America in defiance of the Crown—declared its loyalty to King George but its intense disapproval of parliamentary action and restated the colonists' stand on taxation. It elected William Hooper, Richard Caswell, and Joseph Hewes as delegates to the Continental Congress and put restrictions on trade with Britain. After September 1, they would use no more East India tea; after January 1, 1775, they would import no British goods (including slaves) except medicine; if the whole controversy were not resolved by the following October, they would sell no more naval stores or tobacco to England. To make this agreement even stronger, they declared that anyone not abiding by it would be considered an enemy of the country.

All of this had been men's work, but women in the colony were also involved. It was they who had to find a substitute for British tea. Well, there was sassafras in abundance, which made a lovely spicy red brew, and yaupon, a variety of holly, the Indians of the Outer Banks had used to make a golden tea since before John White's days. In Edenton, a group of women were determined to state their support of the resolutions passed at New Bern.

Tradition says they were headed by Penelope Barker, wife of colonial agent Thomas, and that the "Edenton Tea Party" was held at the home of Mrs. Elizabeth King, whose home bordered the green in front of the handsome red brick Chowan County Courthouse. The day was October 25, 1774, and likely a balmy Indian summer afternoon which allowed them to gather in the Kings' garden, for few houses in Edenton could have entertained fifty-one ladies in their parlors! One by one they signed their names to the agreement "to do everything as far as lies in our power to testify to our sincere adherence" to those resolves.

The news quickly reached London where the *Morning Chronicle* carried it along with a formidable cartoon of the occasion. Arthur Iredell who read it there wrote at once to his brother James, a young Edenton lawyer: "Is there a Female Congress in Edenton, too? I hope not, for we Englishmen are afraid of the male Congress, but if the ladies, who have ever been

esteemed the most formidable enemies . . . should attack us, the most fatal consequence is to be dreaded." The only hope he could see was that probably few places in America "possess so much female artillery as Edenton!"

John Harvey called a second Provincial Congress to meet in New Bern on April 3, 1775. A furious Martin responded by ordering the General Assembly to convene the following day. Members of the Congress included all but one of the fifty-six assemblymen plus twelve

An unusual polished brass snuff box in the governor's bedchamber contains a portrait of George III.

others. Under its moderator, Harvey, the Congress reelected Caswell, Hewes, and Hooper as delegates to Philadelphia and gave full approval to their work at the first session in which a Continental Association had been formed that virtually put an economic boycott on England. They also set up Committees of Safety in each county and town to enforce the decisions of the Continental Congress. Then Speaker of the House Harvey convened the General Assembly, which ceremoniously gave its approval to the Continental Association and other actions of the Continental Congress and reaffirmed the return of its three delegates. Martin addressed them angrily and urged them to resist "the monster, sedition," who "dared to raise his impious head in America." A correspondent for the *New York Journal* of April 27 reported it as "a high-flying, abusive, anti-American speech in which he spoke hard things of all the colonies . . . and people of the continent, except those of his own stamp. . . . " Then the governor wrote Lord Dartmouth that "unless effectual measures . . . are speedily taken, there will not long remain a trace of Britain['s] dominion over the colonies."

In both the east and west, the colony's Safety Committees were already at work, enforcing the resolves of the Congress which, in addition to forbidding British imports, outlawed profiteering and indulging in entertainments. In Rowan County, John and William Kelly were brought before the committee "to answer to a charge of having infringed the Provincial resolve by selling powder at a higher price than it had been sold three months previous." John Oliphant was required to "render an account of some late conduct in opposition to the American measures." In Halifax a merchant who refused to sign the Continental Association's resolves was boycotted by the committee which resolved to have "no commerce or dealing" with him. The Chowan Committee started a fund to encourage local manufacturing and offered special premiums for the production of steel "fit for edged tools." In Pitt County the price of salt was regulated when it started to go too high.

A seventeenth century chess set on a chess table made about 1770 is displayed in the governor's library.

Wilmington's Safety Committee, headed by Cornelius Harnett, was valiant in its support of Congress' warnings against expensive diversions and entertainments in which they included horse racing, dancing, and billiards. After admonishing one group of gentlemen who had organized a horse race, they declared "nothing will so effectually tend to convince the British Parliament that we are in earnest in our opposition to their measures, as a voluntary relinquishment of our favorite amusements. . . . He only is the determined patriot who willingly sacrifices his pleasures on the altar of freedom." They ordered a Mrs. Austin to recall invitations to the ball she was planning, "called up Jonathon Dunbibin for over-charging for salt," encouraged Adam Boyd in his plan to resume publication of the *Cape Fear Mercury,* held public auctions to sell illegally imported goods, warned distilleries about raising the price of rum, and shipped a number of slaves back to their port of embarkation. In addition, they surveyed the quantity of gunpowder on hand within the town and asked local merchants to sell them all that was available and visited "the housekeepers in town" to get their signatures on an agreement to observe congressional regulations.

Such activity alarmed Governor Martin almost as much as the activity of the Continental Congress. It revealed a unity and an allegiance to rebel authority which indicated a withering of the traditions of loyalty to the Crown that had bound the colony and the mother country together more than had the laws. With these ties broken, what was Josiah Martin, he speculated, but a visible symbol of the enemy?

In March he had written to General Thomas Gage in Boston to send arms and ammunition to his aid if troops could not be spared, but his letter was intercepted, and Cornelius Harnett made it public with the comment that "nothing shall be wanting on our part to discredit such diabolical schemes."

In April, realizing its dependency on the colony's naval stores (and possibly deceived by

At the official opening of Tryon Palace in December 1770, the dining room was a blaze of candles as Tryon gave a "very grand and noble entertainment and ball." The Regulators complained of the expense.

Martin's assurances that the colony had more loyal subjects than any other on the continent), Parliament exempted North Carolina from The Restraining Act, a ban on colonial trade with Great Britain or the West Indies which theoretically cut off all European trade as well. The reply of the Wilmington Safety Committee was typical of Harnett's feisty integrity: they rejected it as "a base and mean artifice to reduce them into a desertion of the common cause." In Philadelphia, Will Hooper rejected it just as firmly. His feelings were so well known to his associates that on October 3, when he was late in arriving at Carpenter's Hall, Thomas Willing of Pennsylvania stated firmly from the floor, "North Carolina promises to put themselves in the same situation with the other colonies."

Janet Schaw thought this position was senseless. From Wilmington she wrote home to Scotland, "The ports are soon to be shut up, but this severity is voluntarily imposed by themselves, for they were indulged by Parliament and allowed the exclusive privilege of carrying on trade with Europe. Had the colony taken advantage of this," she said, "they would not only have made great fortunes themselves by being the mart for the whole continent, but they would have had the power to serve the other colonies by providing them in those commodities.... European goods begin to be very scarce and will daily be more so.... I know not what my brother proposes to do with himself or me; for if he stays much longer, he will find himself in a very disagreeable situation. He is just now up the country at a town called New Bern, where Governor Martin resides, whose situation is now most terrible. He is a worthy man by all accounts, but gentle methods will not do with these rustics, and he has not the power to use more spirited means. I wish to God those mistaken notions of moderation to which you adhere at home may not in the end prove cruelty to the mother country as well as these infatuated people."

Josiah Martin's situation *was* desperate. In growing alarm, he sent Elizabeth, who was expecting a baby, and the children to her father's house on Long Island. As some security, he lined up six cannons in front of the palace at New Bern, with powder in the guard room ready at a moment's notice. But New Bern patriots ruined his move—a "motley mob stimulated with liquor" (according to Martin) carried off some of the cannons. Rather than have the rest turned at him, Martin hid them until Abner Nash (his good companion on a trip through the back country in 1772 but now referred to as "a principal promoter of sedition here") came to the palace to request that they be returned to their former positions. He put Nash off with the excuse that he was having new gun carriages made in preparation for saluting the king's birthday in early June, but then, said the governor, he had only inquired as "a mere pretext for insulting me."

In Massachusetts, General Gage also was concerned with the possible arming of the citizenry. Hearing they had stored their powder at a little village called Concord, he marched in the early dawn of April 19 to the village green where Captain John Parker and a small band

Muskets and rifles of Regulators and militia were dusted off as the opposing groups marched to Alamance in May 1771. There Governor Tryon called for a showdown on what had become, in the eastern view, insurrection in the back country.

of Minutemen had been waiting for hours. In a tense moment of confrontation, someone on one side or the other fired his musket, and Sam Adams, leaving in haste from the nearby home of Reverend Jonas Clarke, is said to have exclaimed, "Oh, what a glorious day!"

An express rider pounded down the road from Boston, through Rhode Island and New York, south to New Bern, and from there to the home of William Cray in Onslow County where he arrived at 10:00 a.m. on Sunday, May 7. An hour later, Cray sped a rider on to Cornelius Harnett at Hilton who dashed off a message to Richard Quince at Brunswick:

> I take the liberty of forwarding by express the enclosed papers which were received at three o'clock this afternoon. If you would be at a loss for a horse or a man, the bearer will proceed as far as the Boundary House [on the South Carolina border].
>
> You will please direct it to Mr. Marion or any other gentleman to forward the packet southward with greatest possible dispatch.
>
> I am, Sir, etc.
> Cornelius Harnett
>
> P.S. For God's sake, send the man with the least delay and write Mr. Marion to forward it by night and by day.

Regulators marched from cabins such as this at Merry Hill near Denver.

The colonies were at war! Having aligned herself with their cause wholeheartedly and unreservedly, North Carolina was also at war. There were few illusions left.

In Salem on May 8, several lawyers stopping overnight at the tavern passed along the rumor of a skirmish between British and patriot troops in New England. At services the Moravians prayed for the Continental Congress and studied the text for that day: "When ye shall hear of wars and rumors of wars, be ye not troubled."

In New Bern, Josiah Martin—to whom no express rider had delivered a dispatch—walked the empty room of his Council Chamber, where the laws of King George II and King George III, with the minutes of his Royal Council, still lay on the tables at which his councillors had once sat. The sand sifted slowly down in his hour glass; there was little left of his royal authority. Rumors reached him daily that the Whigs were planning to seize the palace. Where was safety? Perhaps at Fort Johnston with Captain John Collet at the mouth of the Cape Fear River, where an eight gun sloop of the Royal Navy, the *Cruizer*, stood guard offshore.

In the dark of night as the moon rose over the Neuse River, he spiked the palace cannon which had not been carried off. Next, he took two trusted servants and buried what arms and ammunition he could not carry under the deceptively ordinary cabbage patch in the palace kitchen garden. Then, putting out word that he was going to spend a quiet weekend with Chief Justice Hand, he packed a few clothes and rode out the circular cobblestone drive in his carriage—quietly, sedately through New Bern streets, then at the fastest gallop his horses could make to Fort Johnston. From there he issued a proclamation that contained a note of hysteria, threatening death to anyone who attacked him. A few weeks later, as militia deserted the garrison, he took refuge aboard the *Cruizer*. From her decks he watched in the pitch black night of July 19 as Harnett, Howe, and Ashe, with a strong militia force, put the torch to the fort. Furiously, Martin wrote another wordy tirade against them—measuring six feet long and three feet wide! The Provincial Congress declared the only thing suitable for such a document was to have it hanged by the public hangman; then for good measure, they burned it.

Above: In the spring of 1775, time was running out for Governor Josiah Martin as he gazed from the window of the deserted Royal Council Chamber at Tryon Palace. *Right:* On May 24, he buried guns and ammunition under the Palace cabbage patch before his flight to Fort Johnston.

Preceding page:
Statue of General Nathanael Greene
at Guilford Courthouse Battlefield Park.
Below: In the momentous year of 1776,
North Carolinians signed the Halifax
Resolves, the Declaration of Independ-
ence, and the state Constitution.

After Parliament passed its ban on colonial trade, Samuel Johnston wrote a friend in London, "The Ministry... used every opportunity of teasing and fretting the people here as if on purpose to draw them into rebellion.... They have now brought things to a crisis and God knows where it will end."

By the summer of 1775, the end was more apparent. In Rowan County, when word of the battle at Concord and at Lexington was received, the Committee of Safety seized all gunpowder in the county and called for 1,000 volunteers "to be ready at the shortest notice to march out to action."

At Charlotte, Colonel Thomas Polk called a meeting of twenty-seven Mecklenburg leaders, and on May 20, they signed the "Mecklenburg Declaration of Independence," calling themselves a "free and independent people." Records of this signing have been lost, but on May 31 the Mecklenburg Safety Committee passed re-solves declaring all com-missions granted by the Crown "null and void" and asking for an election of officers whose authority would be "independent of Great Britain."

Adam Boyd printed these resolves in the *Cape Fear Mercury*. When the paper reached the *Cruizer*, it almost gave Josiah Mar-tin apoplexy. He dis-patched it to London, saying it "surpassed all the horrid and treasonable publications that the in-flammatory spirits of this continent have yet pro-duced." However, he was still far from hopeless. A Scotsman himself, he pinned his faith on Highlanders near Cross Creek who signed a loyalty oath when they were granted land there, and the Regulators he was sure would rise against the coastal rebels. He evolved a battle plan and sent Alexander Schaw (brother of Janet and Robert) to present it to Lord Dartmouth. He said he would raise as many as 8,000 troops among the Scots and Regulators to march to the coast in February 1776. Here he proposed a rendezvous with General Henry Clinton and 2,000 troops from Boston and Lord Cornwallis who would sail from Ireland with seven regiments in a fleet of fifty-four ships. Together they would reclaim North Carolina and then supply South Carolina Loyalists so Charleston would fall quickly to Clinton's fleet. The Privy Council thought it might work. Meantime from Boston General Thomas Gage sent two Scots officers, Lieutenant Colonel Donald MacDonald and Captain Alexander McLeod, to recruit Carolina Loyalists for the Royal Highland Emigrant Regiment. Martin was overjoyed—here were commanders for his militia! They were to offer Scots who joined them 200 acres of land, tax free for twenty years. He also appointed five Tories to raise troops and march to Brunswick in February.

Following page:
After hearing news of Lexington and Concord,
the Mecklenberg County Committee of Safety declared all Crown commissions
"null and void" and ordered an election of officers "free and independent of Great Britain."
According to tradition, the Resolves were carried to Philadelphia
by Captain James Jack, a Charlotte tavern keeper.

The Wilmington-New Hanover Safety Committee kept these recruiters under surveillance, including James Hepburn of Cumberland who spread the word that 50,000 Russians in his majesty's pay were embarked to subdue America! The committee warned "friends to American liberty" to have no dealings with this "seditious incendiary," and also quickened their pace in recruiting militia and buying arms, ammunition, "drums and colors."

The Provincial Congress, meeting in Hillsborough, authorized two regiments of 500 men each for the Continental Line under Colonels James Moore and Robert Howe and six battalions of 500 Minutemen each.

Janet Schaw watched one of their drills in Wilmington: "Good heavens! What a scene this town is!... I must really laugh when I recollect their figures: 2,000 men in their shirts and trousers, preceded by a very ill-beat drum and a fiddler, who was also in his shirt with a long sword and a cue at his hair. They made indeed a most unmartial appearance. But the worst figure there can shoot from behind a bush and kill a General Wolfe!"

When Gage's officers reached the back country—after giving an oath to Harnett's committee that they were on a social visit—they found two companies already raised by gentlemen of almost their own names: Allan McDonald, and his son-in-law, Alexander McLeod. A well-to-do retired army officer on half-pay, McDonald had great influence with other Scots who in the past few years had built a new life in the rich land along the upper Cape Fear. They and their families had known reprisals, exile, and poverty at home, and while part of their loyalty to the Crown was fear, part was also gratitude. In addition, McDonald's wife, Flora, was beloved by Scots everywhere for helping Bonnie Prince Charlie to escape from the Duke of Cumberland after the Highlanders' defeat at Culloden. What loyal Gael in the Old or New World had not sung the sweet-sad strains of "Charlie is my darlin', the young Chevalier?" or joined with the pipers in celebrating the return of the prince and Flora, the bonny lassie, to Skye?

By the middle of February about 1,300 Highlanders and 200 Regulators had rallied under the king's standard at Cross Creek, but only a third had firearms. The night before they marched, it is said that Flora McDonald, on a beautiful white horse, rode through camp and encouraged the men as bagpipes played their stirring music.

Colonel James Moore, in command of all Whig forces, and 1,100 Continentals fortified the bridge across Rockfish Creek, seven miles below the Loyalists' camp. Donald MacDonald hoped he could bluff his way through the blockade, but Moore also played for time, the two commanders exchanging proclamations from Martin and the Continental Congress and pretending to study them. Meanwhile, MacDonald worked out a plan to bypass Moore. That night, he withdrew to Cross Creek and set out directly east to the coast. Here at the Black River he found his way blocked by Richard Caswell's militia. The canny Scot sent a small group "to amuse Caswell," stationing them among the trees on the riverbank. Here they marched around noisily, bagpipes shrilling, drums beating, and an occasional musket firing as though the army were assembling. Meanwhile, at another point, McLeod constructed a bridge which the Loyalists crossed and marched on eastward. When Moore heard the news, he ordered Caswell to leave at once for Moore's Creek where Alexander Lillington's Wilmington Minutemen would join him. Moore loaded his troops on boats and floated downriver to a point where he could march overland to the Widow Moore's Bridge, about eighteen miles north of Wilmington.

White-haired MacDonald, who was over 70, heard that Caswell had beaten him to the bridge; the old man collapsed from tension and exhaustion. McLeod, more aggressive and impetuous, took command and set daybreak for the attack.

Through the night, Caswell's and Lillington's men worked feverishly. Taking positions across the rapidly moving creek, they removed half the planking on the bridge and greased the log stringers with soft soap and tallow. In the misty light of dawn, under the cypress trees draped in Spanish moss, the Scots were upon the bridge with loud cries of "King George and

Broadswords!" before they discovered its condition. Undaunted, McLeod and Captain John Campbell led the way, steadying themselves on the slippery logs with the tips of their claymores. Almost instantly they were cut down by rifle fire, as were the men closest behind them. Many slid through the missing planks into the creek's black water. The Highlanders were routed within minutes.

A short time later, Colonel MacDonald and about thirty other officers, including Allan McDonald and his two sons, were captured and taken to the Halifax jail. Eight hundred and fifty men were paroled on their pledge not to take up arms against the patriot cause again.

Ezra Stiles, president of Yale, who was traveling in North Carolina, wrote: "The Colonels Moore, Martin, Caswell, Polk, Thackston, and Lillington have great merit; any one of these gentlemen in this country would be an overmatch for a Howe, Burgoyne, or a Clinton. Their knowledge of the country and necessary modes of attack would frustrate any attempt by the characters last mentioned."

With North Carolina's only government an impotent one bobbing at anchor near Brunswick, the Hillsborough Congress in August 1775 had set up a Provincial Council of thirteen members with Cornelius Harnett as president and a complicated structure of delegates. Yet most North Carolinians, like the majority of other colonists, were still protesting the infringement of their rights as "free Englishmen." The Battle of Moore's Creek gave momentum to their desire for independence and a new feeling of confidence in their own forces. John Penn, a thirty-four-year-old lawyer from Granville County who had been named a delegate to the Continental Congress when Richard Caswell became a colonel of militia, now wrote, "The recent events have wholly changed the temper and disposition of the inhabitants that are friends of liberty; all regard or fondness for the king and nation of Britain is gone. A total separation is what they want. Independence is the word most used."

Among those who were not friends of liberty, there had been a change as well. Colonel Robert Palmer of Bath, surveyor-general who had marched with Tryon to Alamance, sailed home to England; so did Judge John Burgwin of Wilmington, treasurer of the colony under Governor Dobbs. Will Hooper stood by, torn with emotion as his brother, Thomas, an avowed Loyalist, left to join others in South Carolina. There were hundreds more who left, alarmed by the rebellious temper of their neighbors which in a few cases had led to Tories being tarred and feathered. A decade ago, nearly all had been devoted subjects of the Crown; it took courage to move in either direction.

On April 4, 1776, the Fourth Provincial Congress convened at Halifax, a borough town for the past sixteen years on the south bank of the Roanoke River. Along the riverfront, small sloops and piroques came and went at the docks loaded with cabbages and corn, hams and tobacco, while large wooden wheels of grist and saw mills turned at an ever increasing pace to meet the needs of its citizen army. Houses of the little town, mostly white clapboard, clustered around the Courthouse Green. Nearby stood the spacious Eagle Hotel, where many of the delegates were staying, and the Masonic Lodge which claimed the distinction of having one of its own members, Colonel Joseph Montfort, as Provincial Grand Master of North America. On the outskirts along Quankey Creek were stately plantation houses framed by sycamore and oak trees, fragrant mock orange, and brilliant crape myrtle. At The Grove, a number of delegates were guests of Whig leader Willie Jones and his new bride, Mary, Colonel Montfort's witty and beautiful daughter, twenty years her husband's junior. The Grove boasted a private circular racetrack where Jones' blooded horses were trained and—to give him a perfect view of it at all times—a paneled dining room at the back of the house with "the largest bay window ever seen in this part of the country." Across the creek, Quankey Place was also crowded with guests, many of whom walked out to inspect the new workshops which Colonel and Mrs. Nicholas Long were having built to produce uniforms and other army supplies under Long's direction as deputy quartermaster general.

Samuel Johnston, moderator of the Congress, faced a long, urgent agenda. He appointed

Harnett to head a committee of seven to consider "usurpations and violences" of the king and Parliament against America and to recommend what measures should be taken. On April 12 the Resolves they had written were read to the Congress and unanimously accepted: "Resolved, that the delegates for this colony in the Continental Congress be impowered to concur with the delegates of other colonies in declaring independency. . . ." North Carolina had now become the first colony to instruct its delegates to vote to dissolve its ties with the British Empire, and thus to vote for a new nation. However, it reserved to itself "the exclusive right of forming a Constitution and law for this colony."

An express rider galloped down cobbled streets and dusty roads to Joseph Hewes in Philadelphia with a copy of the Resolves, and newspapers throughout the thirteen colonies published them with the advice to "follow this laudable example." The next day, Johnston appointed another committee to draft a temporary state constitution; but here there was such a split in opinion that the committee met each night for weeks, after regular sessions of Congress adjourned, burning candle after candle to its socket as they debated. Johnston wrote his brother-in-law James Iredell, "The great difficulty in our way is how to establish a check on the representation of the people to prevent them assuming more power than would be consistent with the liberties of the people," although he admitted this was "a strange piece of patchwork."

Finally, the unresolved question was postponed, and a new statewide Council of Safety set up with Cornelius Harnett as president. He was, in all but title, governor of North Carolina. The Council was to meet continuously; defense of the colony was its principal concern. The need was pressing. Thomas Jones, an Edenton delegate, described the situation to James Iredell: "Our whole time has been taken up here in raising and arming men and making every necessary military arrangement. The word is war, or as Virgil expressed it, 'Bella horrida bella.' Two thousand ministerial troops are in Cape Fear River, 5,000 more hourly expected."

In mid-February, Hewes had sent word to Samuel Johnston from George Washington that General Clinton was in New York, apparently conferring with Governor Tryon before putting out for an invasion of North Carolina in which, the best information reported, he would be joined by the forces of Lord Cornwallis. Only a few days before that letter, Hooper had written Cornelius Harnett, "We now send by the wagon that you directed us to procure, to the care of Samuel Johnston Esq. of Edenton, the drums, colours, fifes, pamphlets [manuals of arms] and a quantity of powder to make up the load." He, too, warned of a spring invasion and urged the Provincial Congress "to counteract the wicked designs of the ministry by providing against the armament intended to destroy your liberties. . . . " Their intelligence was correct. The British forces en route were—belatedly—those Martin had expected in February to rendezvous with his Loyalist troops. While the Halifax convention met, Clinton's ships arrived off Brunswick, but they found no Scots or Regulators cheering from the docks. Colonel James Moore had called out all available militia, including green

Battle of Moore's Creek.
On February 27, 1776,
a group of loyal Highland Scots
charged across the bridge
spanning Moore's Creek. Earlier,
patriot troops had removed half the
planking and greased the stringers
with soap and tallow, defeating the
Scots within minutes.

Far left: Post Road along Moore's Creek where the Scots marched into the patriots' fire; *Center:* Colonel James Moore, who masterminded the successful campaign, took his troops downriver by boat to a rendezvous with General Richard Caswell. *Above:* Diorama at Moore's Creek State Park depicting Highlanders' defeat.

105

The Owens House at Halifax, where in April 1776, the Fourth Provincial Congress drafted resolutions instructing its delegates in Philadelphia to vote for independence, the first of the thirteen colonies to do so.

recruits, and evacuated all noncombatants from Wilmington. By comparison with the British, he still had only a handful of men and had to content himself with harassing outposts and with a glorified guard duty. From April 18 through May 3, the ships of Sir Peter Parker's fleet, with Cornwallis' troops on board, straggled in and the men disembarked, the majority camping near the blackened ruins of Fort Johnston. The frightened residents had fled from Brunswick, and the redcoats avenged the destruction of the fort by indiscriminately burning the neat little houses set among moss-bearded trees which had been hurriedly locked as their owners

left. In the wild illogic of war, they also set fire to St. Philip's Church in which Governors Dobbs and Tryon had worshipped on Sunday mornings. Only its sidewalls of brick remained, the arched window openings staring blindly at the charred homes of the town originally settled by The Family. Apparently to give his soldiers a little additional exercise, Clinton personally led them ashore one night above Orton Plantation where Roger Moore was buried in the family graveyard. They landed at Kendall, Robert Howe's plantation, making so much noise that all they accomplished was a certain amount of looting before being detected by a sentry of William Davis' company of Continentals who shot one Britisher and frightened off the rest before retreating with men and arms intact. As Clinton left, he did manage to burn the Orton Mill and put a torch to Will and Ann Hooper's new house that was still under construction. In a gesture most Carolinians found more humorous than generous, Clinton promised a pardon to all who would affirm their allegiance to good King George—with the exception of Cornelius Harnett and Robert Howe! By the first of June, the fleet hoisted anchor with sixty-three stolen cows and Josiah Martin on board and headed down the coast for Charleston where William Moultrie was waiting for them at Sullivan's Island.

On July 22 an express rider delivered to the Council of Safety at Halifax the electrifying news that on July 4, 1776, the Continental Congress had approved Thomas Jefferson's final draft of a Declaration of Independence "of the thirteen united states of America." Within a week, a wooden platform had been built in front of the Halifax County Courthouse; from it Cornelius Harnett's dockside voice rang out the words from Philadelphia that had already changed the course of North Carolina and all its people. " . . . We hold these truths to be self-evident, that all men are created equal, that they are endowed by their Creator with certain inalienable rights, that among these are life, liberty, and the pursuit of happiness."

When his words died away at the conclusion—to which William Hooper, Joseph Hewes, and John Penn had joined with the other forty-seven signers in pledging "to each other our lives, our fortune, and our sacred honor"—there was a moment of breathless silence. It seemed that not even a dog barked, and no desultory summer breeze stirred a lady's petticoat or the lace on a baby's bonnet. Then a mighty cheer went up that rocked the small crowd of townspeople and those that had ridden in from the country. Moments later they picked Harnett up and carried him jubilantly on their shoulders, 'round and 'round the square. Their cheers reverberated through the green and rustled the leaves of the sycamores along King, Granville, and Dobbs streets. It was a golden day to store up against all the darker ones to follow.

Spurred by a sense of necessity to draw up a state constitution, the fifth and last Provincial Congress gathered in Halifax the following November. A bitter election and debate preceded the drafting of the Constitution. The conservative Whigs, led by Samuel Johnston, James Iredell, William Hooper, Allen Jones, and Archibald Maclaine, stood for a strong executive, property qualifications for voting and office-holding, and few structural changes from the old royal government. On the other side, the radicals, led by Willie Jones (Allen's brother), Griffith Rutherford, and Thomas Person, called for a "simple democracy" with a strong legislative branch and a weak executive subordinate to it. When Thomas Jones of Edenton read the final draft to the Congress on December 6, the radicals had succeeded in shifting the power to the legislature. A Bill of Rights, presented a week later, gave strong assurance against many of the abuses of royal government. Multiple office holding was forbidden, to the delight of the back country. Both the Constitution and Bill of Rights were passed by December 18. The weaknesses of the documents were hardly surprising, for governments are not designed in a few weeks. But the chief cause of future problems lay in the fact that no way for amendment was offered. Thus, any mistakes would be perpetuated for a very long time. Before adjourning, the Congress appointed Richard Caswell as the state's first governor. (Hooper said about the only power he had was to sign a receipt for his own salary!) James Glasgow was made secretary, and a Council of State was selected which included Cornelius Harnett, Thomas Eaton, William Dry, William Haywood, Edward Starkey, and Joseph Leach. Harnett was chosen as Council President.

In early January 1777, Caswell took the oath of office at New Bern in the palace that had been called Tryon's, and a few days later, the first General Assembly of the new state took its seat. . . .

In the years from the Declaration to 1780 colonial leaders struggled to keep spirits up in the face of discouraging odds. The rugged men who for years had sailed the sea and coastal waterways from Edenton, Beaufort, New Bern, Wilmington, and the Outer Banks grew to

Left: Sitting room of the John Wright Stanly House in New Bern, home of the patriot merchant and ship owner who sent privateers to France for munitions, furnished supplies to North Carolina troops at Valley Forge, and is said to have loaned Greene $80,000 for the patriot army. *Below:* the dining room, where a familiar engraving of George Washington and his family hangs above the sideboard.

hero-size in the eyes of the new state as Britain's ships blockaded major ports along the whole Atlantic seaboard. Now their maneuverable little sloops that could slip in and out of shallow inlets and river ports were the lifeblood of trade and supply lines. They sailed south to the West Indies, where cargoes still arrived from southern Europe, and north to carry desperately needed supplies to North Carolina Continentals fighting with Washington. The Outer Banks, which had seemed a barrier, now were a protective reef inside which the unwieldy British men-of-war dared not venture. Deadly fast little privateers slipped through their inlets to prey on British shipping like gnats annoying a lion. Rich cargoes came back to Carolina docks with munitions and merchandise not otherwise available. The missions were dangerous; not all were successful. John Wright Stanly of New Bern lost fourteen privateers. Shipyards rang with the hammering of skilled carpenters. Rope walks and sail lofts kept men at work from dawn till dark. At Edenton, residents fitted out a brig, the *King Tammany,* for defense of Albemarle Sound; two row galleys, the *Caswell* and the *Washington,* were built and stationed at Ocracoke; and the state fitted out the brig *Pennsylvania* with 16 guns and 110 men.

In Philadelphia, Joseph Hewes, whose Quaker upbringing led him to seek a peaceful but honorable reconciliation with England until the final vote for independence, threw himself unstintingly into his work on the Naval and Marine committees. Often he put in twelve hours a day without stopping for food or drink. His experience in the shipping business and his

Left: Interior of the cabin, near Asheville, of Colonel David Vance who fought in the Battle of King's Mountain. *Below:* Rendezvous Mountain, near present-day Wilkesboro, where the militia of Wilkes and Surry counties trained for battle under Colonel Benjamin Cleveland.

shrewd judgment of sailing men were equally valuable. He secured the appointment of senior lieutenant in the new navy for John Paul Jones, who tradition says added "Jones" to his name after he was befriended by Willie Jones of Halifax.

For four years, the Revolution raged beyond North Carolina's borders. The first flush of patriotic fervor had subsided in the state. Caswell and the legislature bickered continually to the despair of North Carolina's members in the Continental Congress and her military men. The governor himself despaired, for he was powerless to balance the requests of his state legislature and the demands of the Continental Congress and General Washington. The North Carolina Continental Line, under General Robert Howe, fought bravely at Brandywine, Germantown, Monmouth and the New York Highlands, Stony Point and the Hudson River. Too often they met defeat or—as at Monmouth—fought to a draw which brought them few laurels. They had suffered at Valley Forge in the terrible winter of 1777-1778, where their feet left bloody footprints in the snow in spite of the efforts by John Wright Stanly at New Bern, Joseph Hewes and Robert Smith in Edenton, and other coastal merchants to keep the men supplied with food and clothing.

Since 1777, Cornelius Harnett had been a member of the Continental Congress, William Hooper having resigned to resume his law practice in order to support his family. Harnett was well aware of the scant pay of a congressman. He wrote his friend Thomas Burke that living in Philadelphia was costing him £6,000 more than his salary with the frighteningly high rate of wartime inflation; but he added, "Do not mention this complaint to any person. I am content to set down with this loss and much more if my country requires it." He grew weary of the quarrels and quibblings of Congress; his "old companion gout" returned as he walked Philadelphia's cold damp streets in winters; he was desperately homesick for the soft breezes of the Cape Fear and the comfort of his own bed. "If I once return to my family," he wrote in a rare moment of despair, "all the devils in hell shall not separate us." In 1779, his friend Joseph Hewes died in his boarding house on Philadelphia's Third Street, an exhausted man, as much a battle casualty as any soldier.

In 1780 the war activity increased. General Clinton, alarmed over the new French-American Alliance which followed on the heels of Burgoyne's surrender to Horatio Gates at Saratoga, decided to move his theater of operations to the south where he felt Loyalist support was strongest. The British commander's new battle plan, which at first succeeded with alarming rapidity, was to take Savannah, then Charleston, and to move north through South Carolina, North Carolina, and Virginia to ultimate victory over all patriot forces. In May 1780, Charleston fell with the surrender of 6,000 American troops, many from North Carolina. In late July, Gates, the hero of Saratoga (whose friends had tried unsuccessfully to promote to Commander-in-Chief as a replacement for Washington), arrived at Coxe's Mill, south of Hillsborough, to take over the pitiful remnants of the southern army. It was a sad, sick army, tick-bitten, oppressed by heat, and suffering from dysentery as a result of a diet of soup thickened with officers' hair powder and green peaches, apples, and corn foraged from Piedmont fields. With incredible optimism, Gates ordered an immediate march on Camden directly through the barren pine forests to the south, even though he had only a few days' rations left. On August 7, 1780, he was reinforced by 2,100 militiamen under General Richard Caswell (Abner Nash had replaced him as governor in April). Caswell warned Gates that his intelligence reports showed Lord Rawdon and British troops at Camden ready to move forward against him. Gates followed the rumor that Cornwallis had marched to Savannah with most of these forces. In truth, Lord Cornwallis had reinforced Rawdon's men.

The night of August 15, the two opposing commanders thought along parallel lines. Each ordered a night march to attack the enemy at dawn. Each ordered the issue of a pre-battle drink to his men—a tot of rum for the British, a gill of molasses for the Continentals. The molasses, on top of the green corn, almost devastated the marching men.

At 2:00 a.m. in darkness black as the hinges of hell, in a clearing between two branches of Gum Swamp, Gates' advance troops literally ran into Cornwallis' advance party moving just as rapidly in the opposite direction! In total confusion, each pulled back for a few hours to reassemble. At dawn Gates gave the order to attack. His totally disorganized army, with

Following page: Battle of King's Mountain.
Cornwallis' southern campaign took a sharp turn on October 7, 1780,
when patriots from North Carolina, South Carolina, Georgia, and Virginia
defeated British Loyalist troops at King's Mountain, South Carolina.
In the bloodiest battle since Bunker Hill,
Colonel Patrick Ferguson was killed,
along with 157 British soldiers and 28 patriots;
nearly 700 British troops were taken prisoner.

untried militia in the front ranks, retreated almost before it advanced. Before an hour had passed, the battle had become a rout with the patriots' retreat led, or so it seemed, by General Gates. He galloped as far as Charlotte that night. At daybreak he set out again and reached Hillsborough with 180 miles and only three and a half days between himself and the battlefield. "What think you of this man?" asked Alexander Hamilton in Washington's headquarters.

The general gloom and despair was broken only by news of harassments to British outposts by raids of young William R. Davie's light horse volunteers. In September, Lord Cornwallis, Banastre Tarleton, his trusted young friend of bloody inclinations, and one Josiah Martin, marched triumphantly to Charlotte. This tiny town, twenty houses scattered along two main streets and a two-story log courthouse at the crossroads, had been anti-British ever since 1772 when the Privy Council refused to grant a charter to its college, Queen's Museum. From behind a wall bordering the courthouse green, Davie's handful of men successfully held off two advances by the British legion, until Cornwallis himself was forced to ride among his troops and shame them into attacking. This third attack was successful in dislodging the insurgents, but Davie's troopers escaped unscathed, more than a little satisfied at their maneuver. Yet Governor Martin was so sure of his welcome that he began issuing proclamations and assurances of "peace and protection to all penitent rebels" and declared the province "rescued, saved, redeemed, and restored."

As Cornwallis marched north, his west flank had been protected by one of his ablest young officers, Lieutenant Colonel Patrick ("Bull Dog") Ferguson, and 1,100 well-trained Loyalist troops. Ferguson, son of a Scottish laird, had held an army commission since he was fifteen. He had become the army's best marksman and had invented a highly sophisticated breech-loading rifle, far superior to any musket in use. He was also impetuous; when partisans of the Appalachians, particularly those under Colonel Isaac Shelby, constantly eluded him after occasional raids on British outposts, he marched boldly to Gilberttown (present day Rutherfordton). Here he paroled a rebel prisoner, Samuel Phillips, and sent him into the Appalachians with the message that if Shelby and his neighbors did not stop their opposition, "he would march over the mountains, hang their leaders, and lay their country waste with fire and sword."

Suddenly the mountain man regarded the war in a new perspective. Isolated by the rugged land, more concerned with protecting his cabin from Indians and wild animals than politics, the frontiersman had never felt the Revolution was as real as his daily battle for food. Some had moved west after Alamance, but most were Scotch-Irish immigrants who came down the Shenandoah Valley in search of land. Here they found it, rich and beautiful. Only when threatened by some intruder, such as Ferguson, did they suddenly become as alert as when their ears caught the sound of a branch snapping or a lonely owl hooting in daytime in the forest. Along the Watauga, the Holston, and the Nolichucky rivers and down from Washington County, Virginia, they came, in buckskins and homespun, hair tied back in a queue under broad-brimmed hats. They packed bags of parched corn and brought jugs of maple syrup or wild honey. Some brought families and friends as far as Sycamore Shoals where they gathered. Here on September 26 they waved goodbye after a proper camp meeting send-off by the Reverend Samuel Doak. He preached a mighty sermon in which he told them how the Lord saved Israel by delivering the powerful Midianites into the hands of Gideon with only a hundred men; he told them to take as their battle cry, "The Sword of the Lord and of Gideon!" Then with Shelby, Colonel William Campbell, and "Nolichucky Jack" Sevier from the Washington District at their head, they rode or hiked over the crest of the Blue Ridge to meet Colonel Bull Dog Ferguson and show him what manner of men he had threatened.

Sometimes the Indian trails they followed through the mountains were almost impassable, but in five days they reached Quaker Meadows. Here they gathered at the home of Colonel Charles McDowell and his brother, Major Joseph ("Quaker Meadows Joe") McDowell, and were joined by their cousin, "Pleasant Gardens Joe" McDowell. The next day, the Surry County men arrived under the command of Major Joseph Winston, whose six brothers also served in the militia, and the Wilkes County partisans of Colonel Benjamin Cleveland, who was said to be the equal of Davy Crockett or Daniel Boone as an Indian fighter and hunter. Cleveland's men had gathered and drilled in a clearing surrounded by rhododendron on top of Rendezvous Mountain, near Mulberry Fields (now Wilkesboro). After resting briefly, all the men marched on, and by October 6 they arrived at the Cowpens just below the South Carolina border, so called because Hiram Saunders, a wealthy Tory, penned his cattle there before driving them to market. That night they enjoyed Mr. Saunders' unintentional hospitality by barbecueing several of his cows, which they acknowledged were of prime grade. After dinner Joseph Kerr, a patriot spy, arrived with the welcome news that Ferguson was only a few miles ahead near King's Mountain. Although a heavy rain had begun, an advance party of about 900 on the best horses available set out in pursuit.

Ferguson had stationed his troops on a fortresslike butte and found time to drop a note to his friend Dr. Tenpenny telling him, "Here we are—kings of King's Mountain." He is said to have added to his officers that God Almighty couldn't drive him from it. On October 7 the mountain men arrived. Having learned that on a steep trail a horse presented too good a target, they hitched their mounts at a distance and moved forward on foot. Keeping well hidden, they surrounded the butte. Shouting "The Sword of the Lord and of Gideon!" they stormed the slope. Ferguson's troops were best at a bayonet charge, and twice they drove the patriots back. But the riflemen fired from behind trees and rocks as they retreated. On the third attack, a group of Shelby's and Campbell's men reached the top. Ferguson's Loyalists, confused by the mountain's incline, continually fired too high, and they had been driven closer and closer together and farther back from the sides each time. When the Loyalists could retreat no farther, the mountain men swarmed up and nearly annihilated them in savage, bitter fighting. King's Mountain was the bloodiest battle since Bunker Hill. Ferguson, blowing his silver whistle in vain to rally his troops, fell from his horse, struck by at least eight rifle balls. In panic, the Loyalists surrendered. They wrapped their commander's body in a green oxhide and buried it, Scottish fashion, beneath a pile of rocks to form a cairn. Many were not buried. Afraid to leave their families unprotected from the Cherokees for even an hour longer than necessary, the mountain men wasted little time on such amenities. The battle won, they turned back to cross the Blue Ridge before the snow drifted too deep through the passes. The British had lost 157 men, the mountaineers 28; 163 Loyalists had been wounded, 62 of the force from over the Appalachians had been wounded; 698 trained men of Cornwallis' forces had been taken prisoner.

Hearing the news at Charlotte, his lordship became physically ill. So did many of his officers. William Davie and his partisans had made life unbearable for them in Mecklenburg County, and Tarleton now called it "a veritable hornet's nest." Cornwallis observed in a letter to Clinton that "Charlotte is an agreeable village, but in a damned rebellious country"; and added that the people there "were more hostile to England than any in America." All things considered, Cornwallis decided to withdraw to Winnsboro, South Carolina. Five miles from Charlotte, he had to abandon thirty supply wagons bogged down in the red clay. They brought great cheer to the patriots who were quick to find them. The British despaired and the Loyalists grew more wary of supporting them, but the news of King's Mountain was like music to Carolina patriots. Those who had grown weary and disheartened as the war had dragged on with defeat after defeat now swelled with pride.

In October, General Nathanael Greene, a 38-year-old Rhode Islander, looked forward to taking command of West Point where his beautiful young wife, Kitty, could join him. Instead, he received orders to leave immediately for North Carolina to take over the southern army from General Gates. He arrived in Charlotte on December 2 and found "only the shadow of an army." Of its 2,457 troops, a mere 1,482 were in camp and fit for duty, and of these only 800 had adequate clothes and equipment. The food supply in Mecklenburg County, already low from Cornwallis' occupation, was nearly exhausted. The brightest news was that General Daniel Morgan, a rifleman from the Virginia backwoods and one of the most effective officers in the Continental Army, had returned to duty in September. Weighing the situation, Greene decided to divide his scant forces. Divided, they could live off the land, and he could post them so that should Cornwallis invade again, Greene could attack on either flank.

Consequently, Greene led his major forces to a camp along the Pee Dee River, just below the Carolina line, while he sent Daniel Morgan with a detachment to move west of Charlotte. He ordered Morgan, who was to be reinforced by North Carolina militia under General William Lee Davidson, to protect that area, to "annoy the enemy in that quarter," and to "spirit up the people." Cornwallis, checking their positions on a map, could see as well as Greene how advantageous this move had been. He quickly planned a countermove. When General Leslie arrived from Charleston with reinforcements, Cornwallis would move north again. Therefore, he sent brash young Banastre Tarleton with his crack dragoons and three battalions from regular regiments in pursuit of Morgan to prevent him from rejoining Greene when the main British force marched forward.

Tarleton and his men—Pennsylvania and New York Loyalists, resplendent in bright green jackets and plumed leather helmets—moved north rapidly to intercept Morgan. However, that brawling veteran of a western tavern town, who, in the French and Indian War, had driven his team of horses over mountain roads with stores for General Braddock, had a devious brain to match his brawn. He left behind scouting parties that Tarleton mistook for his main force and kept cooking fires burning in an abandoned camp, tended by nearby patriots, so his pursuer thought he had left hurriedly within the hour. Lured forward by these deceptions, Tarleton ordered forced marches across rugged country, leaving his troops exhausted. Morgan remained as far ahead as ever. On January 16, Daniel Morgan found the ground that suited him to make a stand—the closely grazed meadow land at Cowpens, dotted with chestnut trees, oaks, and scrub pine, where the mountain men had gathered. Behind him the Broad River, swollen from recent rains, discouraged any untimely retreat.

Cattle graze on a mountainside near Valle Crucis, outside Boone, recalling the unintended munificence of Tory Hiram Saunders who supplied Carolina patriots with a dinner of barbecued beef on the eve of King's Mountain.

Morgan's plan for the next day's battle showed how well the Old Wagoner understood the militia, whom most officers found unmanageable. They were inexperienced, and they were young—many in their teens. Knowing they were the most likely to run in any confrontation, he put them in the front line under Andrew Pickens, an old Indian fighter. Their orders were to move to the rear as soon as they fired three rounds. The men he trusted most—his own riflemen who rallied to his woodsman's turkey call—he assigned to a small skirmish line well in front. Compared to Tarleton's regalia the riflemen were laughable in their homespun hunting shirts, battered tricorn hats often with a coon's tail pinned in back, powderhorns over their shoulders, and a hunting knife or tomahawk in their belts. But any one of them could easily shoot a knot out of a piece of wood at 150 paces. The seasoned Continentals, under John Eager Howard, were to be hidden from view in the second line. Morgan had few cavalry, so he picked fifty militia and mounted them on the best of the sorry old farm horses they had ridden into camp. In a third line at the rear, Morgan put the cavalry alongside his company of mounted militia.

That night, after carefully explaining the battle plan to his officers, Morgan walked into the woods alone. There in the darkness which fell early on the short January days, he climbed a tall tree and, as he later wrote to a friend, "poured out my soul in prayer for protection."

One member of the militia, Thomas Young, remembered that night. "He [Morgan] went among the Volunteers, helped them with their swords, joked with them about their sweethearts, told them to keep in good spirits, and the day would be ours. And long after I laid down, he was going among the soldiers, encouraging them, and telling them the Old Wagoner would crack his whip over Ban in the morning as sure as he lived. . . . I don't believe he slept a wink that night." The forty-eight-year-old Morgan may not have slept. The cold damp weather and the many nights of bivouac on icy ground had brought on an attack of his old tormentors, sciatica and rheumatism, so that he had trouble even mounting his horse. His troops, however, had both uninterrupted rest and a good breakfast the morning of January 18 before Morgan drew them up in ranks. With a touch of showmanship, he bared his back— scarred in purple ridges from 499 lashes from a British whip, applied for having a fist-fight with a lieutenant in the French and Indian War. As he had intended, his amazed men grew hot with the thought of British tyranny. Then they took their places and waited until Tarleton and his weary and hungry troops, who had been marching since two o'clock that morning, appeared.

Morgan galloped along the line calling, "They give us the British halloo, boys—give them the Indian halloo, by God!" The militia and riflemen fired and fell back on signal. Tarleton's dragoons, taking this for a retreat, rushed forward into the stronghold of the Continentals. Morgan rallied the militia again. "Form, form, my brave fellows! Give them one more brisk fire and the day is ours! Old Morgan was never beaten!" As the militia re-formed and William Washington's mounted troops surged forward, the British broke in panic. When the smoke drifted off the Tory's cow pasture, Tarleton had lost 10 officers and 100 men, with

Sparked by his riflemen, General Daniel Morgan defeated Colonel Banastre Tarleton at Cowpens, South Carolina, in January 1781.

twice that number wounded, and 500 to 600 taken prisoner. In addition, Morgan's troops had resupplied themselves with 800 badly needed muskets, a traveling forge, 35 wagons, 100 horses, and "all the music." Since the latter belonged to the 71st Highlanders, their bagpipes would surely add a new sound to "Yankee Doodle."

The exhilarating news of the victory at Cowpens that reached Greene's camp on the Pee Dee five days later was celebrated in high spirits with a *feu de joie*—the traditional firing of guns and what Colonel Otho Williams called "an operation of some cherry bounce." The jubilant Greene decided to set off at once on horseback with a sergeant's guard to ride the hundred miles to Morgan's camp where they could plan their next moves. He left General Isaac Huger to move up the main body of troops at an easier pace. As he cantered north, Greene reflected on how this war was unlike a textbook war and how this very fact worked against the well-trained British soldiers. The Carolina back country that he rode through was wild, wooded, and largely uninhabited. It was criss-crossed with streams and rivers. Such roads as there were had been rutted and frozen, their red clay often covered with pine needles which had grown slippery with heavy rain until the roads were not so much mud as morasses. But the back country men of the militia knew the lay of the land like a Bostonian knew his city streets.

The stocky, ruddy-faced New Englander had prepared himself for this campaign by learning everything he could of North Carolina's topography. He sent out exploring parties as soon as he arrived to supplement the few existing maps with reports on the various rivers and fords, the availability of boats, and the distance between towns on what roads there were. He absorbed the information so well that young General Davidson, a native Carolinian from the Charlotte area, remarked that Greene knew more about the Catawba than many men who had been raised on its banks.

Here and there Greene passed a small isolated farm, its fields lying fallow for the winter, a milk cow penned up near the house to keep her from wandering in the path of foragers of either army, and a few scraggly chickens pecking in the dirt. The rough little cabins of hewn logs, cracks filled with native clay, looked strange to Greene's Rhode Island eye and added to his feeling of isolation in a foreign land. For the most part, the cabins were of one or two rooms with one door, one window with a wooden shutter closed against the January chill. Their roofs were fashioned with split timbers, and a pale blue finger of smoke reached upward from their chimneys. Greene sighed as he pulled his coat tighter around him to keep out the wind. He reminded himself that the tides of war—his war, at any rate—had changed at last at Cowpens.

That winter was one North Carolinians would talk about for years. Albemarle Sound froze for the first time in anyone's memory, and a man in Chowan County walked out thirteen miles on solid ice. In the Piedmont, the December and January days and nights had been an unbroken sequence of icy, penetrating cold. The damp, miserable weather made a man long for a roaring fire with a kettle bubbling on its crane and a hearty drink in his mug. There had been days when Greene had almost wished for a good clean New England snow to turn the world white and fresh again.

Greene heard that Leslie's troops had now reinforced General Cornwallis. He knew that he could not overpower their combined strength, that he must outwit them. The chess game was on, and in a way he anticipated it gleefully. He had learned from his general the famous Fabian strategy of tempting the enemy to battle but never joining it. This strategy had served Washington well in the northern states. Finesse would have to do what force could not.

On January 30, Greene eased his saddle-sore body into Daniel Mogan's tent on the east side of the Catawba at Sherrard's Ford just as Cornwallis' men reached the western shore. As Greene warmed himself in the Old Wagoner's account of his rout of Tarleton at Cowpens, the British stared in dismay at the Catawba, frothing and roiling menacingly at its banks. The flooded river between the redcoats and Morgan's troops was as impregnable as a fort.

"Providence!" cried some, and patriot newspapers from Charleston to Boston so reported it.

"Carolina!" grinned others, wise in the ways of Piedmont rivers.

The next day the muddy water began to recede, and Greene sent Morgan eastward to safety with his troops. He assigned General Davidson and his militia to determine which ford Cornwallis was most likely to cross when the river fell and to carry on a delaying action to give Morgan a headstart toward the Yadkin. Then they were to rendezvous with Greene on the road to Salisbury. At 1:00 a.m. on February first, Cornwallis decided the Catawba had receded far enough for him to brave the current, the stony river bottom, and the 500 yards of rapid, muddy water. He chose Cowan's Ford as his crossing point.

Sixteen-year-old Robert Henry was among the North Carolina militia. After fighting at King's Mountain, he had decided to put down his borrowed musket and go back to his school books. This he did until Robert Beatty, his lame schoolmaster, heard that Cornwallis was camped only seven miles from the school. He dismissed the class, took up his rifle, and marched off to join Davidson's men. Robert Henry and five of his friends, reinforced by a half-pint of whiskey which they bought for a one hundred dollar Continental bill, hiked the mile and a half to Cowan's Ford to fight alongside their teacher. Here, the boys bedded down, but not before Henry spotted a projecting rock. He reasoned that if the enemy got as close as the rock, he would run.

In the black hours before dawn, as Henry and his buddies slept, Cornwallis' Tory scout, Dick Beal, lost his bearings at the unexpected sight of Davidson's watchfires and accidentally led the British into deep water. The schoolboy woke with a start to hear the sounds of men and horses wading through water unexpectedly over their heads.

Robert Henry wrote: "[Joel] Jetton, having a fine voice, cried, 'The British! the British!' . . . By the time I was ready to fire, the rest of the guard had fired. I then heard the British splashing and making a noise as if drowning. I fired and continued firing, until I saw that one on horseback had passed my rock in the river, and saw that it was Dick Beal, moving his gun from [over] his shoulder, I expected, to shoot me. I ran with full speed up the bank."

He was stopped in mid-flight by the sight of his schoolmaster, hit by a British bullet that broke his thigh bone. "He fell," the teenager recalled, "still halloaing for me to run."

A Tory with Cornwallis also gave a vivid description of the scene. "For a while I saw 'em hollerin' and a-snortin' and a-drownin' — and the river was full of 'em a-snortin', a-hollerin' and a-drownin' until his Lordship reached the off bank; then the rebels made straight shirt tails and all was silent. . . . "

But before his lordship reached that bank, his horse had been shot from under him, as

In the bitter winter of 1780–1781, British and American armies nearly marched themselves out of shoes. The Salem shoemaker was sorely pressed by large orders from Cornwallis and Greene and found it impossible to fill either.

had been the horses of Generals O'Hara and Leslie. What caused the rebels to "make straight shirt tails" was not the enemy—it was the bullet fired from midstream (some said by the Tory Beal) that struck their beloved General Davidson as he was momentarily silhouetted against the flickering yellow flame of a watchfire. Davidson died instantly, and the disheartened North Carolina men and boys who had rallied under him—their skirmish won, and the conflict moving eastward from their own land—dispersed into the darkness, "going home," as Greene reported despairingly to his commander-in-chief, "to tell the news." The next day, ten miles downstream, a beaver hat was discovered floating on the Catawba, its hat band inscribed, "Property of Josiah Martin, Governor."

As a gray, rainy dawn broke, Greene waited nervously at David Cain's farm, the rendezvous point. Where was Davidson? Where were the militia? When the dreadful word arrived, it took all Greene's strength to mount his horse and head on to Salisbury alone. He arrived at Steele's Tavern at noon and slowly swung himself out of his saddle. He was limping more than usual, his leg was aching from the long ride, and the deeper ache of defeat flowed through him. An army doctor caring for prisoners there met him at the tavern door.

"How are you, General?" he asked in concern.

"Tired, hungry, alone, and penniless," Greene is said to have replied. Elizabeth Steele, the innkeeper, overheard him and hurried to bring him a hot meal. Then, as the story is told,

In February 1781, Morgan led his troops safely across the rain-swollen Yadkin River only hours before the British arrived to find its banks flooded and the river impossible to cross.

Cornwallis' soldiers occupied the Michael Braun House at Granite Quarry, south of Salisbury, in the winter of 1780–1781; here the British held American prisoners.

she pulled two well-worn leather bags from the pocket under her apron and handed them to the weary general. In them were her life savings.

"You need these," she told him, "and I can live without them." Money could not bring back men, but for Nathanael Greene at this moment, it was not only a symbol of faith but the entire sum of his military funds. When he set out again a few hours later to join Morgan, the rain was coming down harder, unceasingly. He knew that in Carolina this meant the rivers would flood in another two days. He must get his men across the Yadkin before then.

As Greene sped across the Piedmont between the rising rivers, the Moravians—buffeted between opposing armies—recorded the drama as it unfolded.

February 2, 1781 — Bethania. Meat was provided for 600 British soldiers taken prisoner at Cowpens.

February 3, 1781 — Salem. Three wagons from the town and three from the country must be furnished to help move the [patriot] powder magazine from Salem.

On February 3, the Americans were safely on the east side of the Yadkin as the river rose. A few hours after the last boat was pulled ashore, General O'Hara and the British advance

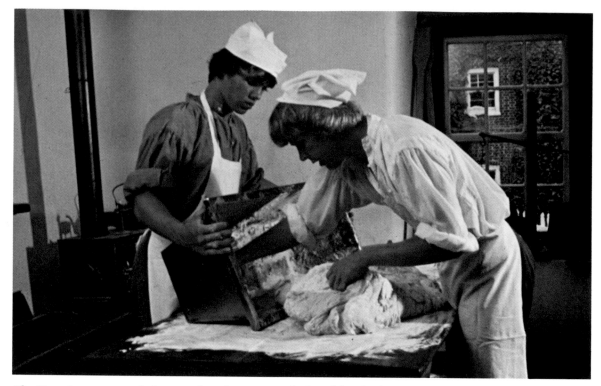

The Moravians were caught in a crossfire of requisitions for bread from both armies. When Cornwallis finally crossed the Yadkin, he arrived in Bethania and sent orders to Salem for bread and all the flour the mill could grind.

guard arrived at full gallop. Once again, between them and the patriot army lay an impossible stretch of white water. By the time the Yadkin began to recede, Morgan was marching his troops toward Guilford Courthouse and a rendezvous with Huger. The devious Greene was headed north in a feint to lead Cornwallis to believe he planned to cross the upper fords of the Dan River into Virginia. His lordship obligingly took the bait, knowing that Greene was anticipating reinforcements from the Old Dominion. As soon as Greene had word that the British were committed to a northward march, he headed east for Guilford Courthouse.

February 6, 1781 — Bethabara. During the night, General Pickens arrived with his men and something over 20 wagons. Corn, hay, bread, and brandy were given to him at his request.

February 8, 1781 — Bethania. Yesterday and today many wagons have passed, with whites and blacks fleeing to Virginia. This evening we heard that the English army under General Cornwallis had passed the Shallow Ford [of the Yadkin] about three o'clock.

February 9, 1781 — Bethabara. . . . about eleven o'clock a company of English dragoons arrived, bringing an order from Lord Cornwallis for brandy, meat, meal and bread and instructions that our mill would grind all it could, and that in the afternoon our wagon should take it to Bethania where there were 7,000 men. A guard hailed someone at the tavern: "Good friend." Reply: "Whose friend?" Answer: "King George's."

February 9, 1781 — Bethania. About noon, the English really arrived here. Threats were given if 20 horses were not produced by six o'clock, so the boys put in charge of

In March 1781, Nathanael Greene's troops met the British army under General Cornwallis at Guilford Courthouse. Although the American flag was hauled down in defeat, it was said in England that "another such victory would ruin the British army!" The patriot flag carried at Guilford Courthouse was photographed at Tryon Palace.

gathering them got 11 from the town and stole 6 from the English teamsters, turning them in as part of the Bethania requisition.

February 10 — Salem. Major Ross announced that Lord Cornwallis would stop for a while with Brother Bagge, which he did soon after, with him being General Leslie, McCloud, Major England, and Governor Martin.

At Guilford Courthouse, Morgan waited for Greene with a 44-year-old body that refused to obey his spirit which was still as young as when he took on all comers in Battletown twenty years before. Spasms of sciatica doubled him over in agony; he suffered the misery and indignity of piles; he tossed and turned in his tent. Even his jaw ached — that scarred lower left jaw stripped of its teeth by an Indian's bullet years ago. Morgan had no choice. He must go home and recuperate. His pain equaled the humiliation he felt at having to tell Greene he could not accept command of the detachment that was to lead Cornwallis on a false trail while the main body of troops crossed the Dan River at the lower fords.

Colonel Otho Williams took Morgan's command, and the ruse worked. Greene made straight for the Dan, preceded by Thaddeus Kosciuszko and a small detachment who were to get the boats ready. On February 14, Greene's forces crossed safely into Virginia, and Williams' men followed in such jubilation that the happy echo of their shouts drifted across the water, sending a chill through General O'Hara and his advance British troops. Their fears were realized as they gazed across the river where Kosciuszko was securing the last of the boats. . . .

Having been denied a military victory, or even a strategic one such as Greene's, Cornwallis decided to make a political move. He and Royal Governor Josiah Martin would move into Hillsborough and raise the royal standard. Surely in this Regulator stronghold, the

Loyalists would rise *en masse* to welcome him. His hopes proved vain. The royal standard fluttered in front of the courthouse, but few arrived to salute it. The streets were so muddy that he set some of his soldiers to work laying paving stones. Less than a week later he was forced to move out, having eaten Hillsborough out of all its food, including the tough steaks from freshly butchered oxen which local farmers had counted on for their spring plowing.

Nathanael Greene, reinforced by troops from Virginia, recrossed the Dan and after two weeks of skirmishing with small groups of Cornwallis' soldiers, marched to Guilford Courthouse. With the two armies encamped each night close to one another, the early weeks of March demanded special vigilance. Greene set up a routine for himself. As soon as each day's march ended, he wrote official reports and letters then caught a few hours of desperately needed sleep. Several hours before dawn when the danger of attack was greatest he would arise and make a personal round of his sentry posts to be sure that all was quiet. One morning before daybreak as he passed the tent of a young staff officer, he heard the loud rumble of snoring which gave no doubt that its occupant was fast asleep. This struck the conscientious Greene as being so irresponsible that he burst into the tent and shook the snoring officer. As the young man opened heavy eyelids, Greene snapped at him, "How can you possibly sleep at this hour when Cornwallis could attack at any moment?"

With perfect confidence the young officer murmured, "But, General, I knew you were awake!" In retrospect, Nathanael Greene realized this was probably the highest compliment he could be paid.

At Guilford, Greene waited to do battle with the British who were only a few miles south at New Garden. Numerous Quaker families lived in the area, and Greene—whose Quaker upbringing was never far below the surface—met many of them and arranged for them to nurse his sick and wounded. One group, realizing a major battle was in the making, promised to join in prayer throughout its duration. Greene was deeply touched.

Nathanael Greene prepared his plans for the coming engagement in much the same way Morgan had done at Cowpens. Only one element was missing, Morgan's rough homespun spirit. His ability to talk to militia in their own language and inspire them with a fierce personal loyalty could never be equaled by Greene, quiet, reserved, intellectual, with little confidence in militia. Still, he did his best to ask of them no more than they could give and to offset with careful planning the element of charisma which surrounded the Old Wagoner.

Guilford provided the classic battlefield on which British veterans were trained. Its little courthouse stood on a rise at one end of the ground. The fields and woods below were bisected by the road the English would travel. Here Greene stationed his men and waited until the enemy arrived, an awe-inspiring sight "with banners and a most gorgeous array," bagpipes shrilling and drums beating.

Like Morgan's militia, the first line of Greene's young recruits had been told to fall back after the first three rounds of fire, but when they broke, it was not an orderly retreat to a new

Graveyards like the Old Burying Ground at Beaufort bear mute testimony to the cost of independence. Buried here are Colonel William Thompson, highest ranking patriot officer from Beaufort, an unknown Revolutionary War Continental soldier, and an anonymous British Naval officer who begged not to be buried "with his boots off." He was buried standing up as his poignant marker attests.

position but a rout. Their confused flight immobilized the experienced men drawn up behind them, leaving no clear line of fire or even space to maneuver their horses. Cornwallis' men pushed forward. Here they met the Continentals and officers of the militia, who, furious and frustrated at their inability to rally and regroup their own troops, turned back to join the battle. "I never saw such fighting since God made me," Cornwallis cried. Realizing he was about to lose every man of his crack regiments in the hand-to-hand massacre, he made a desperate move. He ordered his artillery to be turned on the bloody struggle before him. Both sides reeled back. From that point on, it was a matter of tactics as to who withdrew first. Greene, seeing his line of retreat rapidly being cut off, opted to take his men out of danger. This left Cornwallis on the field but with losses so great that when word reached England, Charles James Fox exclaimed, "Another such victory would ruin the British army."

All of Greene's horses were dead, so his heavy artillery had to be left on the battlefield among the wounded and dying men. The skies literally opened, and torrential rains drenched them all. Down the road to Reedy Fork Greene marched through the mud with his troops. After ten miles, they found a safe bivouac on the shore of Troublesome Creek. Here he walked among the exhausted soldiers as they dug out breastworks in case Cornwallis pursued them. Then Nathanael Greene—the resolute, weary man who had not taken off his stained uniform in six weeks, who had been a Quaker, a lover of peace, for his first thirty years—stumbled into his tent and fainted.

On April 7, Cornwallis fell back to Wilmington where he moved into the magnolia-shaded weatherboard house which Judge John Burgwin had built. Major James Craig had located his headquarters there since invading the city in late January. Here Cornwallis hoped to rest and resupply his troops. After that, he planned to march back to South Carolina and consolidate his forces with those of Lord Rawdon in Camden. However, news of Greene's next move foiled even this possibility. Realizing how vulnerable the British hold on South Carolina was with Cornwallis in Wilmington, General Greene turned south quickly toward Camden.

The British commander knew he faced a crisis, and a speedy decision was necessary. Since he could not reach Camden before the Americans did, he elected instead to move into Virginia and join forces with Benedict Arnold. And so he marched to Virginia and a few months later to Yorktown where for the first time his drum beat retreat. Lieutenant Ebenezer Denny was there by the York River on that bright October day. He wrote, "I never heard a drum equal to it—the most delightful music to us all. . . ."

For that steadfast member of the Sons of Liberty Cornelius Harnett, the music came too late. In February, he had ridden home from the Continental Congress in Philadelphia, sick and frail from repeated attacks of gout. At Wilmington, he found his old friend John Ashe, Brigadier General of militia, trying to recruit an indifferent handful of men, weary of war, tired of defeat. When Craig and his men came ashore, those few stout-hearted militia who still

After the Battle of Guilford Courthouse, Cornwallis marched to Wilmington where he made his headquarters at the Burgwin-Wright House, now home of the North Carolina chapter of the Colonial Dames. *Left:* Spring flowers adorn the hall table under the portrait of Judge John Burgwin. A Loyalist, Burgwin had been colonial treasurer under Governor Arthur Dobbs whose portrait hangs in the library *right. Below:* The beautiful boxwood garden at the rear of the house.

rallied around the aging Ashe and the ailing Harnett did their best to rescue the New Hanover military stores for the American cause. But the boats they loaded with ammunition and sailed up the Cape Fear were ill-fated. Some were captured, and two others went aground in shallow water where their crews burned them to keep them from enemy hands. Harnett had been entrusted with a large sum of money to buy additional supplies. When he got word of Craig's approach, he saddled his horse and set out to carry the money to safety. He accomplished his mission, but as he rode through Onslow County, another attack of gout seized him. He painfully reached the plantation home of Colonel James Spicer. There Craig's men tracked him and arrested him. Harnett was unable to walk or ride, so they tied his hands and feet with rope and threw him across the back of a horse like a sack of grain. At Wilmington—where he had once led the strongest resistance in the colony—they dumped him into a roofless blockhouse. For weeks, spring rains soaked him, and alternately a merciless sun beat down. The day after Cornwallis left Wilmington, Cornelius Harnett was dead. He had requested that no elaborate funeral be held, as he thought it unfitting in a time of war to spend money on such ceremony. In accordance with his wishes, he was buried quietly in the shaded churchyard of St. James. He had chosen his own epitaph, two lines from Alexander Pope:

> *Slave to no sect, he took no private road,*
> *But looked through Nature up to Nature's God.*

John Ashe, who fifteen years before had told Governor Tryon that North Carolinians would fight the injustices of the king "to the death," joined those others who did so. His hiding place betrayed, he was captured by Craig and shot as he tried to escape. Still sick from his wound, he was thrown into prison where he contracted smallpox. He was paroled to his home in Clinton but died there only a few days later.

Peace and independence were bought at no bargain prices in North Carolina. Cornwallis' defeat and surrender at Yorktown, October 18, 1781, did not mark the end of atrocities. The Tories, encouraged by Major Craig, grew bloodthirsty and such bands as "Scaldhead David" Fanning's terrorized the countryside and burned houses from the Cape Fear to the Piedmont. At Hillsborough, they kidnapped Governor Thomas Burke and spirited him out of the state. Nevertheless, all this was aftermath; the war, for all practical purposes, was over.

The 12th
Star in a
New Flag

The John Wright Stanly House in New Bern.

When Governor Alexander Martin presented to the General Assembly of North Carolina a copy of the Treaty of Paris which officially ended the American Revolutionary War, he concluded expansively, "Nothing now remains but to enjoy the fruits of uninterrupted Constitutional freedom."

His reaction was natural after eight long years of war. Peace had seemed to offer the solution to the problems of a people divided against itself, of weak and inefficient state and local govern-

ments, of inflation and economic depression. Unfortunately, peace was not a panacea.

The problems facing the new state of North Carolina were legency relief gion. Emerfor the hunwas required Carolina padreds of North prisoner since triots held of Charleston the battles den. Compenand of Camfinancial and sation for the rifices of vetpersonal sacto be made. erans needed settlers in the western part

of the state needed to be met. The status of the Loyalists and of their property needed attention.

In 1783, Governor Martin was able to announce the successful negotiation for exchange of war prisoners. General Greene had been a great help in this endeavor. As a result of this agreement, when the British evacuated Charleston, the North Carolinians commenced their journey homeward.

The state wished to repay these soldiers but the treasury was depleted. Instead the state's wealth was measured in its vast expanse of western lands. Consequently, portions of this territory were granted to veterans in amounts varying according to the rank each man held. The veterans received bonuses ranging from 640 acres for a private soldier up to 12,000 acres for a brigadier general.

A great westward movement began, but this in itself did not provide a total solution. The need for improved transportation became more urgent, and the new western settler was quick to demand that the state increase protection from the Cherokees and locate courts closer than that at Morganton, located on the eastern side of the Blue Ridge.

North Carolina discussed dispensing with the demands of the settlers in the western part of the state by the cession of the transmontane region to the new federal government formed under the Articles of Confederation (effective 1781). Many of the westerners favored cession as did some easterners who saw themselves thus relieved of the expense of governing that region. Others foresaw the possibility of the federal congress requesting taxes from the states on the basis of population. (Congress did not have the authority to levy taxes.) The subsequent expense of a populous western area was another argument for cession. Still another group held out for retaining the western land and selling it to pay off the state debt.

In the spring of 1784, the legislature passed a Cession Act, but Conservatives led by William R. Davie protested so vigorously that within five months it was repealed. It was five more years before North Carolina again ceded its transmontane land to the United States.

The legal matters pertaining to the state's Loyalists were more easily settled than the animosity between Whigs and Tories who continued to dwell side by side when peace came. In 1777, and 1779, the state had passed Confiscation Acts under which property of known Loyalists was taken and sold, and the money was directed into the meager state treasury. Radical Whigs urged that this policy be continued after the war's end, while both Moderates like Martin and Caswell and Conservatives like Johnston and Hooper urged a policy of conciliation. In 1783, the Assembly passed an Act of Pardon and Oblivion, but its terms were harsh. Those Tories who had served as officers or who had left the state, often to fight under British officers, and some additional groups were denied pardon.

Despised by their neighbors and harassed by their government, hundreds of Loyalists moved from North Carolina to Nova Scotia, Florida, England, and Scotland. Sadly, many of them were still men without a country in their new homes. Some had been born in the American colony and remained forever homesick for North Carolina.

In 1786, a North Carolina state court made a landmark decision in the case of Baard vs. Singleton: it declared a 1785 statute based on Confiscation Acts unconstitutional. It was the first time a legislative act had been ruled in conflict with a written constitution.

Although humanitarian considerations were of primary importance, the efficiency of the governmental body could not be disregarded. The state capital, after eight years at Tryon Palace in New Bern, had reverted in 1778 to the earlier tradition of moving from town to town at the discretion of the governor. Once again the state records joggled from hither to yon in a cart, a practice printer James Davis had deplored in the years before Tryon Palace was built. The temporary capital moved from Hillsborough to Halifax, to Smithfield, Fayetteville, New Bern, Tarboro, and Wake Court House. The residents of each town loudly proclaimed its virtue as a permanent seat of government, and a few political factions lined up with each proponent. Those from Fayetteville seemed to be leading when, ironically, a location that was not a town at all—"within ten miles of Isaac Hunter's plantation in Wake County"— suddenly swung into popular favor in 1788. The furious and nonplussed losers proclaimed that such a site "would never rise above the degree of a village." Nevertheless, within a few years a commission purchased 1,000 acres of land from plantation owner Joel Lane, and the

The dining room of the James Iredell House in Edenton. Iredell married Hannah Johnston, sister of Governor Samuel Johnston whose portrait hangs above the mantle. The two Edenton Federalists helped lead the fight for ratification of the United States Constitution.

city of Raleigh was laid out, named in honor of that nobleman's attempt at colonization 200 years previously. Contrary to predictions, Raleigh rose above village status in due time.

Less pragmatic but perhaps more important than a location for the state capital was the threat presented by the weaknesses in the Articles of Confederation. These weaknesses, which Cornelius Harnett had foreseen, became increasingly evident in the five years after the war. The new central government had no power to levy taxes or regulate commerce, it had no judicial or executive branch, and it could not authoritatively deal with foreign nations because each treaty had to be separately ratified by thirteen state legislatures.

Trade barriers had sprung up between the states, and public credit had reached a low ebb. Inflation was growing, and no united effort could be made to curb it.

The state's Conservatives (many of them plantation owners, merchants, and professional men who had stood in the forefront of the Revolutionary movement) called for a new federal constitution. North Carolina Radicals (the majority from the central or western part of the state) were mostly small farmers. In the tradition of the Regulators, many distrusted the east and demanded personal liberty, paper money, and few taxes. The Radicals did not want a strong, distant national government. They preferred a government easily controlled by individual citizens, particularly farmers. This group was by far in the majority in the population of North Carolina which then stood at about 350,000.

The kitchen-dining room of the Vance Birthplace near Weaverville. After the war, when ratification was a burning issue, the homes of eastern and western citizens were as different as their owners' points of view.

Unfortunately, all but one of the delegates selected to represent North Carolina at the Constitutional Convention were from the east. At that first meeting in 1787, not one represented the interest of the man on the lower rungs of the socioeconomic ladder. Willie Jones of Halifax, who headed the Radical cause, had declined to serve as a delegate.

Those who rode to Philadelphia from North Carolina to help hammer out a new form of government were Hugh Williamson, a brilliant scholar and physician from Edenton; William R. Davie, a war hero from Halifax; Richard Dobbs Spaight, nephew of the late Governor Arthur Dobbs and from New Bern; Alexander Martin from the Piedmont area; and William Blount from Windsor. All had served in the Revolutionary forces, all were well educated and experienced in politics, all (except Williamson) were slave owners, an economic rather than a moral distinction in that day. None had calluses from plowing a rocky field or wielding a hammer, none wore homespun hunting shirts, none had crossed the mountains to carve out a farm or build a cabin. Perhaps a frontiersman could not have brought legal education or expertise to the difficult task of working out the fine points of a constitution. But he could have contributed support and understanding of the new Constitution once he returned to North Carolina, if he had taken part in approving its provisions as compromises were made.

Dr. Williamson provided the delegation's leadership in Philadelphia. He made seventy-three speeches at the convention and was tireless in his work on five separate committees.

Preceding page: Fog hangs over the Pioneer Homestead at dawn in Smoky Mountain National Park near Cherokee. *Left:* Magnolia blooms on the western lands granted to veterans of the Revolution.

Davie, a quiet man, represented the state on the important Grand Committee that worked out the Great Compromise which resulted in a bicameral legislature for the United States Congress with representation being equal in the Senate and based on population in the House of Representatives. With their constituents' old fear of a powerful executive, the entire delegation opposed the plan for a president who would not be voted on by state legislatures; moreover, they opposed the admission of new states on an equal basis with the original ones. Their objections were typical of the entire convention. There was unanimous agreement on only one point—the need for writing a constitution with which men of all opinions could live and under which a new nation could deal with powerful, established countries. In this larger goal they succeeded.

Francis Hopkinson, the Philadelphia patriot whose witty song lyrics had enlivened many a trying moment during the Revolution, penned a serious ode for the Fourth of July, 1788, that summed up the problems and accomplishments of the convention and ended with a plea for ratification of the Constitution:

> *... My sons for freedom fought, not fought in vain;*
> *But found a naked goddess was their gain;*
> *Good government alone can shew the maid*
> *In robes of social happiness arrayed.*
> *Hail to this festival ! all hail the day !*
> *Columbia's standard on her roof display:*
> *And let the people's motto ever be*
> *United thus, and thus united Free.*

When North Carolina's signers returned from Philadelphia, their welcome was a far cry from the one that had greeted the signers of the Declaration of Independence a little more than a decade previously. The state was torn with political dissension, name calling, and stump speeches that resembled those in a modern primary election campaign. New parties were formed—the Conservatives now being known as Federalists and the Radicals as Anti-Federalists. Somewhere between came the views of the Moderates. Anti-Federalists loomed large on the political scene: Timothy Bloodworth, a Wilmington blacksmith, and farmers and craftsmen like Samuel Spencer, Matthew Locke, and Thomas Person. All of them declared that the proposed Constitution was a dangerous document. Most colorful of those who harangued the precincts was the Reverend Lemeul Burkitt. He proclaimed that the proposed Federal City known as the "ten-mile square," would be an enormous armed fort from which legions of soldiers would march out to quell dissidents. Such erstwhile heroes as Washington and John Adams, he declared, would turn the government into a monarchy and deliver it to France so all its citizens would be forced to become Roman Catholics!

The Federalists, too conservative by nature to dip their pens quite so deeply in vitriolic fantasy, still were not above referring to Anti-Federalists as a "blind, stupid set that wish

Colonel David Vance, a veteran of Germantown, Brandywine, Valley Forge, King's Mountain, and Cowpens, built his homestead about 1790 near Weaverville. His farm in Rim's Creek Valley was the earliest settlement in the Blue Ridge; his grandson, Zebulon B. Vance, later governor, was born here in 1830.

Following page:
At the Polk Farm south of Charlotte,
Samuel and Jane Knox Polk started
married life on Christmas Day, 1794.
Their son, James, eleventh President
of the United States, was born the
following year.

Hayes Plantation in Edenton was built by Samuel Johnston, Revolutionary leader and governor during most of the debate over the Constitution. In the left wing, as seen above, is Johnston's remarkable library containing over 5,000 volumes.

damnation to their country" or, as did Archibald Maclaine, calling them "knaves and fools." William Hooper admitted that he "distrusted the common people" whose votes "could always be purchased by a drink of toddy."

As the debate on the Constitution wore on, rational opponents based their case on the lack of a Bill of Rights. Such rights had been won at too great a cost, said the Anti-Federalists, to be forgotten now, and they refused to sign a constitution with such a serious deficiency. When the convention to ratify the Constitution met in Hillsborough in 1788, those opposed to ratification met the solid opposition of Federalists. These men foresaw that unless a workable system of cooperation was formed among the states, that unless those who had fought for liberty would agree they were interdependent on one another, no victory had been won.

Nevertheless, even the statesmanlike pleas of James Iredell for a "united vigorous government" to cure the "disordered and distracted" condition of the country would not turn the tide of votes. The result was a sweeping 184 to 83 count against adoption.

For almost a year, North Carolina stood as an independent state against eleven states aligned under the new Constitution. (Rhode Island had also failed to ratify it.) Federalists led by James Iredell embarked on a powerful educational campaign to explain the advantages the new Constitution would bring to the state and its citizens. Faced with the potential cost of federal tariffs on North Carolina trade and the instability of paper money being issued by the

In the Johnston library, the busts over the mantle are George Washington (top) and (below) John Jay and John Marshall. Portraits left to right are John Stanly, son of John Wright Stanly of New Bern; Peter Brown, lawyer; and James Iredell, Jr., governor in 1827–1828.

Anti-Federalist legislature and the inflation it caused, a majority of voters began to favor the Federalist viewpoint. By the following year, when James Madison introduced the Bills of Rights in Congress and ratification of these Constitutional amendments by the individual states was underway, the opposition of back country farmers had diminished.

When a new convention to consider ratification met in Fayetteville in November, 1789, the vote to ratify the new Constitution was carried overwhelmingly.

As soon as word reached him, James Iredell sent a rider to Edenton with the news. The next morning the townspeople gathered on the green in front of the Chowan County Courthouse as the dawn broke over a cold blue bay. The flag rose on its pole by jerky inches; at last it reached the top, and the autumn breeze from over Albemarle Sound caught and flung it out in full beauty. James Iredell's dream had come full circle, as many an immigrant boy's had done and would do in the next decades. It had cost many the full measure, and their spirits were also felt there on that frosty morning in the shadows of the green: Cornelius Harnett, James Moore, John Ashe, and others of The Family, Joseph Hewes, Penelope and Thomas Barker, Nathanael Greene, and the schoolboy Robert Henry, Daniel Morgan, and William Davidson, and all the nameless others who had brought North Carolina to this day. For these the flag streamed in the wind, and North Carolina's second two hundred years began.

July the Fourth has been celebrated at Salem since 1783
when Governor Alexander Martin decreed it would be observed statewide as a day of thanksgiving.
The traditional ceremony includes an evening procession past illuminated houses
climaxing with music sung by two antiphonal choirs.

SOURCES AND ACKNOWLEDGMENTS

The photographer and author deeply appreciate the immeasurable help of numerous people throughout North Carolina. We received invaluable cooperation from directors of historic sites, individuals who welcomed us into their homes, and many persons who shared their interest in North Carolina's heritage. Among those who helped make this book possible, our special thanks go to: the North Carolina Bicentennial staff in state headquarters at Raleigh and in the many cities we visited; National Park Service staffs at Roanoke Island, King's Mountain, and Guilford Courthouse; Nancy and John Gilliam Wood of Hayes Plantation; Donald Taylor of Tryon Palace; Anne Cross of Bethabera; Frances Griffin of Old Salem; Lou Hafermehl; Mary Hadley Griffin; Alda Todd; Ida Kellam; and John Tyler.

Agniel, Lucien. *The Late Affair Has Almost Broke my Heart.* Riverside, Conn.: Chatham Press, Inc., 1972.

Asbury, Francis. *The Journal of the Rev. Francis Asbury* vol. I. New York: N. Bangs & T. Mason, 1821.

Ashe, Samuel A. *Biographical History of North Carolina,* 8 vol. Greensboro, N.C.: C. L. Van Noppen, 1905–1917.

Bowen, Catherine Drinker. *John Adams and the American Revolution.* Boston: Little, Brown & Co., 1950.

Brawley, James S. *Rowan County: A Brief History.* Raleigh: North Carolina Division of Archives & History, 1974.

Butterfield, Lyman H., ed. *Diary and Autobiography of John Adams.* Cambridge, Mass.: Harvard University Press, 1961.

Fries, Adelaide, *et al.* ed. *Records of the Moravians in North Carolina.* Raleigh: North Carolina Division of Archives & History, 1922–1969.

————. *The Road to Salem.* Chapel Hill: University of North Carolina Press, 1944.

Greene, George Washington. *The Life of Nathanael Greene.* New York: Hurd and Houghton, 1871.

Hayes Library Collection. Hayes Plantation, Edenton, N.C.

Historic Edenton Collection, Edenton, N.C.

Hudson, Arthur Palmer. *Songs of the Carolina Charter Colonists.* Raleigh: North Carolina Division of Archives & History, 1962.

Lawson, John. *A History of North Carolina.* London: 1709, 1714. Reprinted, Charlotte Observer Printing House, 1903.

Lee, E. Lawrence. *Indian Wars in North Carolina (1663–1673).* Raleigh: North Carolina Division of Archives & History, 1968.

Lefler, Hugh T., ed. *North Carolina History told by Contemporaries.* Chapel Hill: University of North Carolina Press, 1965.

———— and Albert R. Newsome. *North Carolina—The History of a Southern State.* Chapel Hill: University of North Carolina Press, 1954–1973.

———— and William S. Powell. *Colonial North Carolina.* New York: Charles Scribner's Sons, 1973.

McEachern, Leora H. and Isabel M. Williams, eds. *Wilmington—New Hanover Safety Committee Minutes, 1774–1776.* Wilmington, N.C.: New Hanover County American Revolution Bicentennial Association, 1974.

MacNeill, Ben Dixon. *The Hatterasman.* Winston-Salem, N.C.: John F. Blair Publisher, 1958.

Meyer, Duane. *The Highland Scots in North Carolina.* Raleigh: North Carolina Division of Archives & History, 1963. Reprint 1968.

Moore, Frank. *Diary of the American Revolution.* Edited by John A. Scott. New York: Washington Square Press, 1967.

Parramore, Thomas C. *Cradle of the Colony.* Edenton, N.C.: Edenton Chamber of Commerce, 1967.

Paschal, Herbert R., Jr. *A History of Colonial Bath.* Raleigh: Edwards & Broughton Co., 1955.

Porter, Charles W., III. *Adventurers to a New World.* Washington, D.C.: National Park Service, 1972.

Powell, William S. *The Proprietors of Carolina.* Raleigh: North Carolina Division of Archives & History, 1968.

Rankin, Hugh F. *The American Revolution.* New York: Capricorn Books, 1965.

————. *The North Carolina Continentals.* Chapel Hill: University of North Carolina Press, 1971.

————. *The Pirates of Colonial North Carolina.* Raleigh: North Carolina Division of Archives & History, 1972.

Robinson, Blackwell P. *The Five Royal Governors of North Carolina.* Raleigh: North Carolina Division of Archives & History, 1968.

Ross, Malcolm. *The Cape Fear.* New York: Holt, Rinehart & Winston, 1965.

Schaw, Janet. *The Journal of a Lady of Quality.* Edited by E. W. Andrews and C. M. Andrews. New Haven: Yale University Press, 1923.

Stick, David. *The Outer Banks of North Carolina.* Chapel Hill: University of North Carolina Press, 1958.

Stember, Sol. *The Bicentennial Guide to the American Revolution,* vol. 3. New York: E. P. Dutton & Co., Inc., 1974.

Treacy, M. F. *Prelude to Yorktown.* Chapel Hill: University of North Carolina Press, 1973.

Tryon Palace Collection, New Bern, N.C.

Wertenbaker, Thomas J. *Norfolk—Historic Southern Port.* Edited by Marvin V. Schlegel. Durham: Duke University Press, 1962.

INDEX